Johan

You are very precious to God

100 daily readings for the pre-teens, with **100** fun-packed riddles and challenges

Lux Verbi.BM

For
Louise, Dirkie and Marli.
You are precious
to God and to
your father and mother.

Originally published in Afrikaans under the title:
Vir God is jy baie kosbaar
Copyright © 2001 Lux Verbi.BM

Copyright English edition
You are precious to God © 2001 Lux Verbi.BM
P.O. Box 5, Wellington 7654
South Africa

All rights reserved

No part of this book may be reproduced
in any manner without prior written permission from the publisher.

All Scripture quotations, unless otherwise indicated,
are taken from the Holy Bible, New International Version (NIV).
Copyright © 1973, 1978, 1984 by International Bible Society.
Used with permission.

Translated by M. Strydom

Typesetting by Lux Verbi.BM

Printed and bound by
NBD/Paarl Print
Drukkery Street, Cape Town
South Africa

First edition, first print 2001

ISBN 0 7963 0037 2

Contents

A. You are very special to God — 7

1. God gives you his promises — 8
2. God made you very special — 10
3. Children are precious to God — 12
4. God knows your name — 14
5. God wants you to be joyful all the time — 16
6. God knows what is going to happen to you today — 18
7. You are worth a lot to God — 20
8. Praise God because He is the Creator — 22
9. God's love for you is unconditional — 24
10. God is holding your future in his hands — 26
11. Jesus sets you free — 28
12. God wants you to rest sometimes — 30
13. God holds you close to his heart — 32
14. God made you for a unique purpose — 34
15. You are a winner — 36

B. God wants to bless you with wonderful relationships — 39

16. God wants you to honour your parents — 40
17. Jesus wants you to forgive other people — 42
18. God wants you to choose your friends carefully — 44
19. God wants you to have good friends — 46
20. Your family is precious to God — 48
21. You can help others — 50
22. You can be a good friend — 52
23. Your parents can also make mistakes — 54
24. God will bless you in his own time with a special boyfriend or girlfriend — 56
25. God gives us sex, but it can also be dangerous. — 58

C. God is always with you — 61

26. God takes care of you — 62
27. God is always with you — 64
28. You need never be afraid — 66
29. You belong to the King — 68
30. God holds your hand tightly — 70
31. God always listens to you — 72
32. Emmanuel: God is with you — 74

D. God wants you to grow spiritually — 77

33. You can talk to God — 78
34. God gives you his whole creation — 80
35. God gives you his Word — 82
36. You want to tell — 84
37. God gives you the spiritual food to grow — 86
38. The Bible is your light — 88
39. Jesus wants to use you — 90
40. You can make time for God — 92
41. Other people are also precious to God — 94
42. You can help with the harvest — 96

E. God is asking you to be faithful — 99

43. You can make your own choices — 100
44. God doesn't want you to use foul language — 102
45. God wants you to live like Jesus — 104
46. God is waiting for you at the finishing line — 106
47. God wants you to speak the truth all the time — 108
48. You need not be a chameleon — 110
49. God wants you to live according to your beliefs — 112
50. God wants you to think before you speak — 114
51. You are a house in which God is living — 116
52. God wants you to build your life on Him — 118

F. God is with you when you are going through a hard time — 121

53. Hand your crisis over to God — 122
54. A crisis can make you strong — 124
55. You can be joyful even though are going through a bad time — 126
56. God carries you when you are going through a bad time — 128
57. Suffering is not God's punishment for you — 130
58. Suffering can be your own fault — 132
59. God sees your tears — 134
60. It isn't always easy to be a Christian — 136

G. The cross is meant for you — 139

61. The cross is meant for you — 140
62. God loves you so much that ... — 142
63. The cross is for forgiveness — 144
64. God wants you to believe in Jesus — 146
65. God's gift to you is eternal life — 148
66. God wants you to be certain that you are going to heaven — 150
67. Jesus makes you brand new — 152
68. God loved you first — 154
69. Only the blood of Jesus brings forgiveness — 156
70. We can't buy or earn redemption — 158

H. You are just as precious as... — 161

71. You are just as precious as Joseph was — 162
72. You are just as precious as Jeremiah was — 164
73. You are just as precious as Noah was — 166
74. You are just as precious as Daniel was — 168
75. You are just as precious as David was — 170
76. You are just as precious as Gideon was — 172
77. You are just as precious as Asa was — 174

78. You are just as precious as Samuel was — 176
79. You are just as precious as Timothy was — 178
80. You are just as precious as Elijah was — 180

1. Promises from God to you — 183

81. A promise that God's redemption is for ever — 184
82. A promise that God is always with you — 186
83. A promise that God hears and answers your prayers — 188
84. A promise that God is not ashamed of you — 190
85. A promise that nothing can separate you from God's love — 192
86. A promise that God gives you hope — 194
87. A promise that God's Word is for ever — 196
88. A promise that your words can make a difference — 198
89. A promise that the Lord will bless you if you speak the truth — 200
90. A promise that you will be blessed if you honour your parents — 202
91. A promise that God will bless your charity — 204
92. A promise that God can make you able — 206
93. A promise of peace when you do the right thing — 208
94. A promise that God will help you in times of temptation — 210
95. A promise that the Lord determines your future — 212
96. A promise that the right friends will be a blessing to you — 214
97. A promise that God will keep you safe — 216
98. A promise of blessing when you are faithful to God — 218
99. A promise that God will comfort you when you are sad — 220
100. A promise that God will never leave you alone — 222

You are very special to God!

Isn't it absolutely wonderful to know that you have a special place in someone's heart?
Think about all the times when your father or mother spoils you or when a friend gives you a card to say how special you are. It makes your heart feel nice and warm inside, doesn't it?
In the following 15 daily readings you are going to learn how incredibly special you are to God. Yes, you, small as you are, are very special to the great, almighty God. You need not try to understand it. You need not ask why this should be so. Only know that it is true. Believe it, enjoy it and live it!
Enjoy each of the daily readings, learn from them what is important and remember to read the Bible text with each daily reading until you know it by heart. It is not hard, and it will change your life forever.

God gives you his promises

People often make promises which they do not keep. Even friends make promises they don't keep. It is even worse when your father or mother promised that they would play with you for an hour of so, or would take you out to dinner, and something comes in between. You have looked forward to spending precious time with them and now you are very disappointed. Later on you find it hard to believe people who make promises all the time, but do not keep them. Perhaps you have also made promises that you did not keep.

The good news is: God never breaks his promises. When God promises something, He makes them come true. There are thousands of promises in the Bible that God gives to his children. Especially during times when things are not going so well and you are desperate, you can rely on God's promises – because He makes them come true.

The Lord tells you in 2 Timothy 2:13 that He is faithful and that He will keep his promises. Yes, even when you are unfaithful and disobedient, God's promises stay true. God really is faithful!

God has made you very special

Nearly every week you can watch some beauty contest on the TV or read about it in the newspapers. If it is not Miss South Africa, it is Mr South Africa or Miss Tinkerbell. You even read about schools having beauty contests, like Miss Valentine or Mr Athletic. At school many children also receive prizes for various achievements. The heroes and heroines of the school are the beautiful, the clever and those who are good at sport. And perhaps you are the one sitting on your own, feeling sad and thinking: I am just not good enough. I am stupid, ugly and a good-for-nothing.

In Psalm 139:13 God says that He has formed each one of us in a very special way. God definitely has not forgotten about you or simply left you out. No, He made you beautiful and good. That is why you must praise Him. God does not see us as we are from the outside. To excel in sport and to be pretty are not important to God. He sees what is in your heart. You can know for certain: God made you special and He made you for Himself.

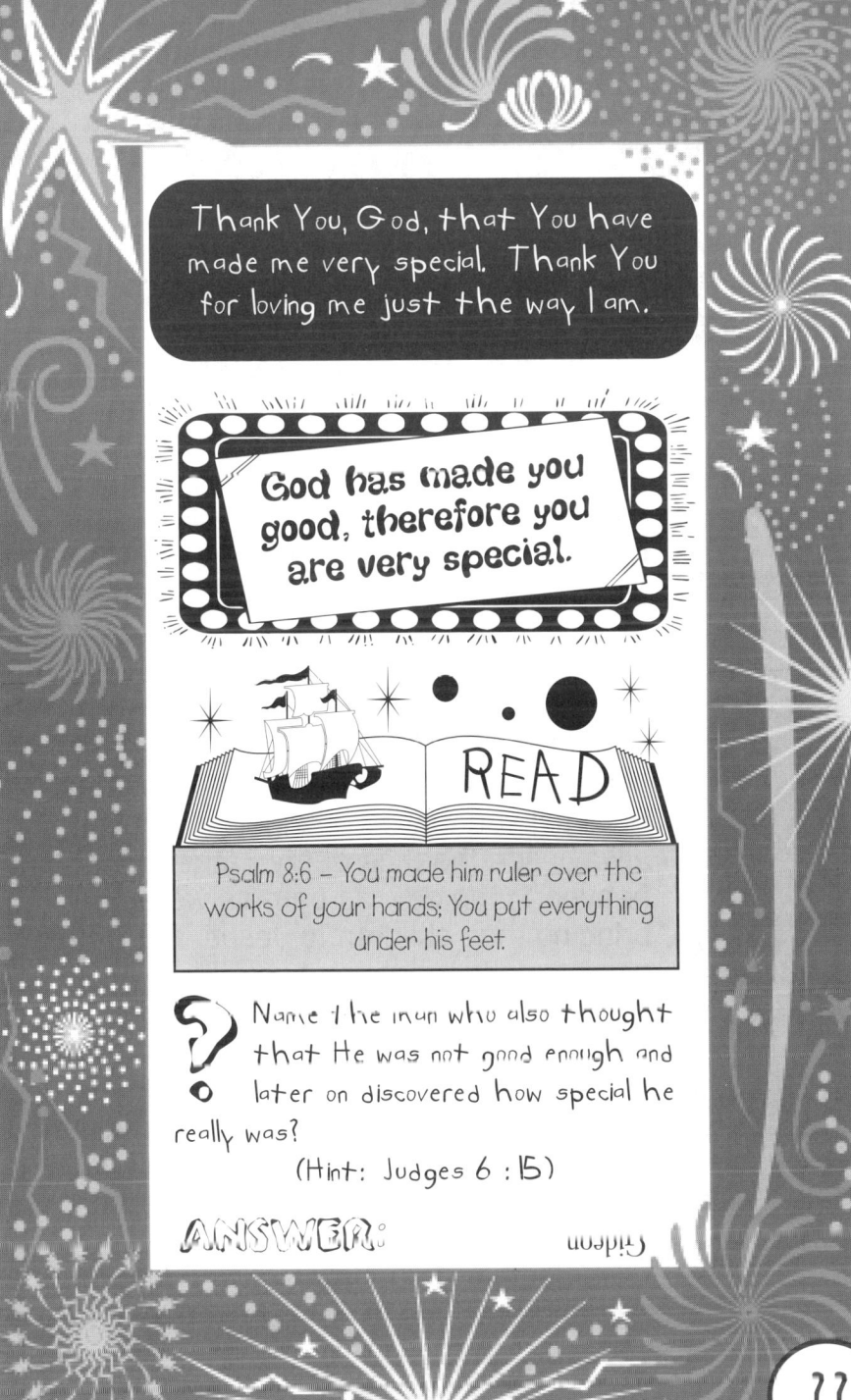

Thank You, God, that You have made me very special. Thank You for loving me just the way I am.

God has made you good, therefore you are very special.

READ

Psalm 8:6 – You made him ruler over the works of your hands; You put everything under his feet.

Name the man who also thought that He was not good enough and later on discovered how special he really was?

(Hint: Judges 6:15)

ANSWER: Gideon

Children are precious to God

Jack was complaining to his mother, "Mum, children never count. This wedding invitation also says: 'Sorry, no children'. And do you remember that last year we could not even go to the party at Dad's work?"

"Son, I know you get the feeling that children are not important, but that is not the real reason why people put it on this wedding invitation. And even though you might not be important to some people, there is One to Whom children are very important – and that is God."

Matthew 18:10 says, "See that you do not look down on one of these little ones. For I tell you that their angels in heaven always see the face of my Father in heaven." One day, as parents were bringing their children to Jesus, the disciples chased them away. They thought that his other work was more important than these children. They even thought that the people were in the way and were wasting Jesus' time by bringing their children to Him. But Jesus scolded his disciples and immediately gave the children his full attention.

Remember: You are also very important and precious to Jesus, even though you are young.

God knows your name

"Why did you and Dad give me such a strange name?" Sara-Mari asked her mother. "Most people can't remember what my name is and no-one knows how to spell it."

"You know that you have been named after Grandmother Sarah and Grandmother Mary," her mother replied. "But remember, even though people sometimes forget your name, there is Someone who will never forget it, and that Someone is the Lord. Whether you are Ingmar Ingverstadt from Sweden or Kgalaletso Rakau from South Africa, God knows your name."

Because God made you so unique and because you are so special to Him, He knows your name. In Psalm 139:1-2 we read, "O Lord, you have searched me and you know me. You know when I sit and when I rise; you perceive my thoughts from afar." God has known you since before you were born.

Doesn't it make you feel very special to know that God knows your name and can even count the number of hairs on your head?

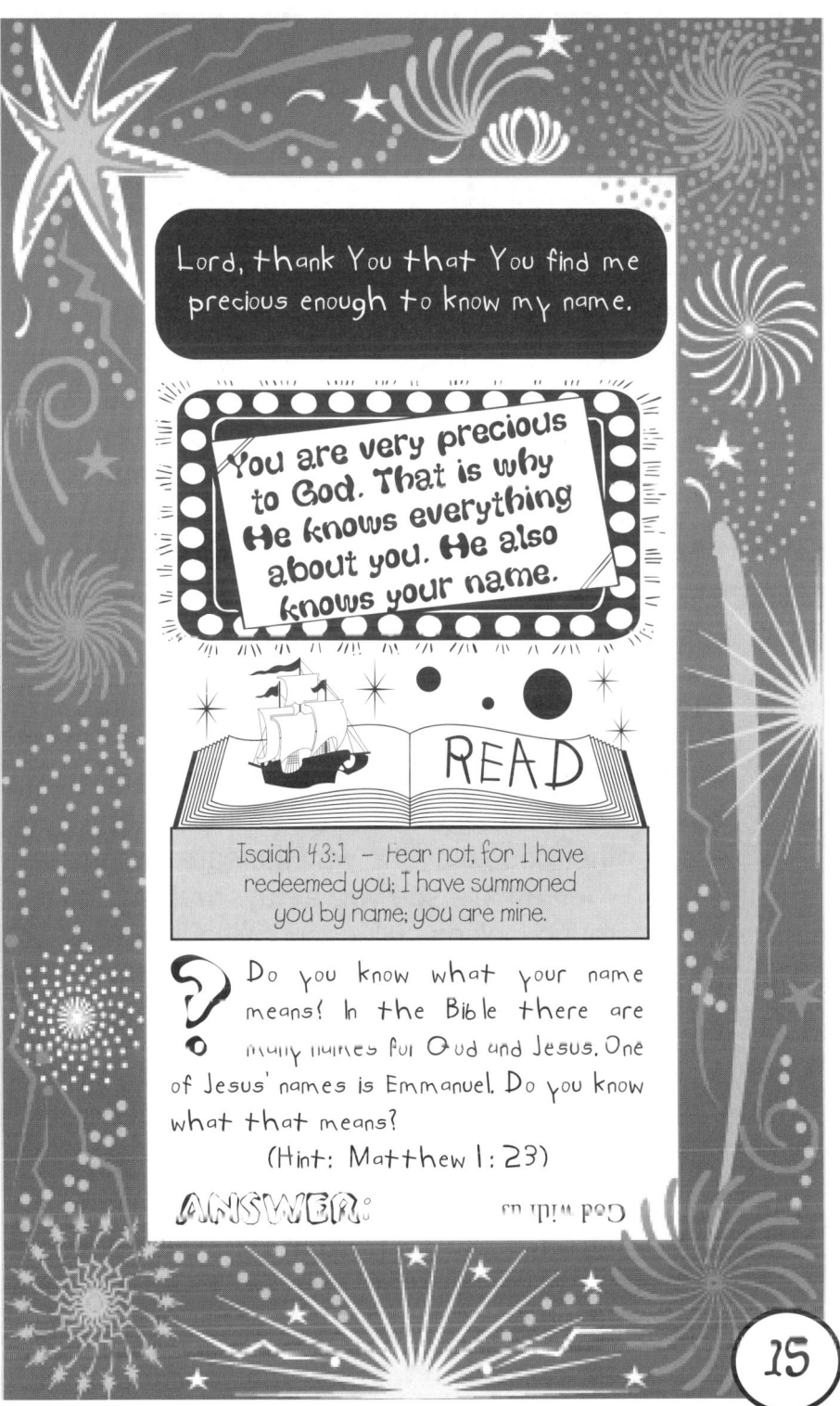

Lord, thank You that You find me precious enough to know my name.

You are very precious to God. That is why He knows everything about you. He also knows your name.

READ

Isaiah 43:1 — Fear not, for I have redeemed you; I have summoned you by name; you are mine.

? Do you know what your name means? In the Bible there are many names for God and Jesus. One of Jesus' names is Emmanuel. Do you know what that means?

(Hint: Matthew 1:23)

ANSWER: God with us

15

God wants you to be joyful all the time

Penny was talking to her schoolteacher. "You know, Miss, I find it fantastic that you are always so cheerful," she said. "The children in our class are very naughty, but as soon as you have scolded us, you are cheerful and friendly again. How do you do it?"

"Penny, sometimes it is very hard to be cheerful. Sometimes I do not feel well and sometimes I am angry and not in the mood to be cheerful. But when I think about how much the Lord loves me and how special I am to Him, I can't help being cheerful and happy."

Children of God act as examples to other people by the way they are living. When people see you always walking around looking sulky and sullen, even though you claim to be a Christian, they won't have any desire to be children of God too.

Think of a few reasons for being cheerful and happy when you are a child of God. One such a reason is that one day you will be with God in heaven. Another reason is that God is with you all the time and is taking care of you. Is this not reason enough to be happy?

God knows what is going to happen to you today

Mister Cohen, an old man, lived near a small coffee-shop. Every morning, for the past thirty years, he went there to have his breakfast. Every morning the waitress asked him, "What are you having today?"

Every morning Mister Cohen only smiled and said, "Whatever you are serving this morning."

Mister Cohen knew this coffee-shop so well that he was sure they would not serve him any kind of rubbish. They always made his breakfast exactly as he liked it.

Sometimes your life is the same as the scene described in that coffee-shop. Everything happens exactly the way you think it should. You get up in the morning, go to school, do your homework, take part in sport, watch TV and go to bed at night. But now and then something very bad happens to you. People disappoint you or your plans fail. Isn't it good to know that God decides what you have on your menu every day?

He plans your life in such a way that, whatever happens, it is good for you in the end. He is with you every day – even in bad times. He holds your whole future in his hand.

You are worth a lot to God

On a very busy day young Cliff visited the supermarket with his mother. They walked around the shop buying some of the things they still needed for the dinner they were planning for their neighbours. Suddenly Cliff saw something shiny lying on the ground under one of the shelves. He quickly picked it up. He showed it to his mother. Her eyes grew big, because it was a beautiful diamond ring that Cliff had picked up. It had to be worth thousands of rand. When they reached the security guard of the supermarket, they found a woman there, crying bitterly. The moment she saw her ring, she gave Cliff a big hug of joy and R50 as a reward.

There are many things in our lives that are worth a lot to us, like diamond rings, expensive cars and exotic, imported food. But what does God consider worthy? You … yes, you are worth a lot to God.

Matthew 10:31 says that to God you are worth a lot. Nothing or no-one is more precious to Him than you are. Know this: You are God's most valuable possession.

Lord, thank You that I am worth a lot to You. Thank You that even if I sometimes do not feel so worthy, I can be certain that this is not true. I am your most valuable possession.

You are worth a lot to God, just as you are.

READ

Matthew 10:31 – So don't be afraid; you are worth more than many sparrows.

Write down some of the things in your homes that cost a lot of money and are very valuable. Then finally, write down your name as God's most valuable and most precious possession.

God's most precious possession:

Praise God because He is the Creator

One evening at dinner Gerald said, "Gee, Mum, people are so clever. On TV today I saw someone win R500 000 in a quiz show."

"Yes, but have you thought about how wonderful God is? It is He who made those clever people," his mother answered.

People nowadays are very clever. They can make the most wonderful things – aeroplanes, spacecraft, computers and many other things. But sometimes we forget that only God is able to create. He can make something out of nothing. He can make things that grow and live. Look at the blue sky, the sea, the mountains. Didn't God make the world beautiful? Praise the Lord for this beautiful world.

The most wonderful thing God created is man. God created man to rule the world. Genesis 2:26 tells us so. You have emotions and you can think. Praise God because He made man – and you too – so wonderful.

God's love for you is unconditional

John was sitting in class, quietly doing his homework. Some of the other children were not behaving, even though Miss July had asked them to be good while she was in the headmaster's office. The noise was growing louder. John tried to make them keep quiet, but they wouldn't listen. The next moment Miss July stood in the doorway. "Can't you be quiet even for five minutes? I asked you so nicely. John, thank you for being so good. I love you very much …"

"And what about us?" asked Gerald.

"Not when you are making such a noise and are behaving so badly, Gerald," Miss July answered.

This story teaches you what conditional love is. The teacher loved the children on the condition that they kept quiet. God's love works very differently. Whether you are good or bad, pretty or ugly, fat or thin, God loves you unconditionally.

1 John 4:16 tells us that God is love. He loves you unconditionally in spite of who you are or what you do.

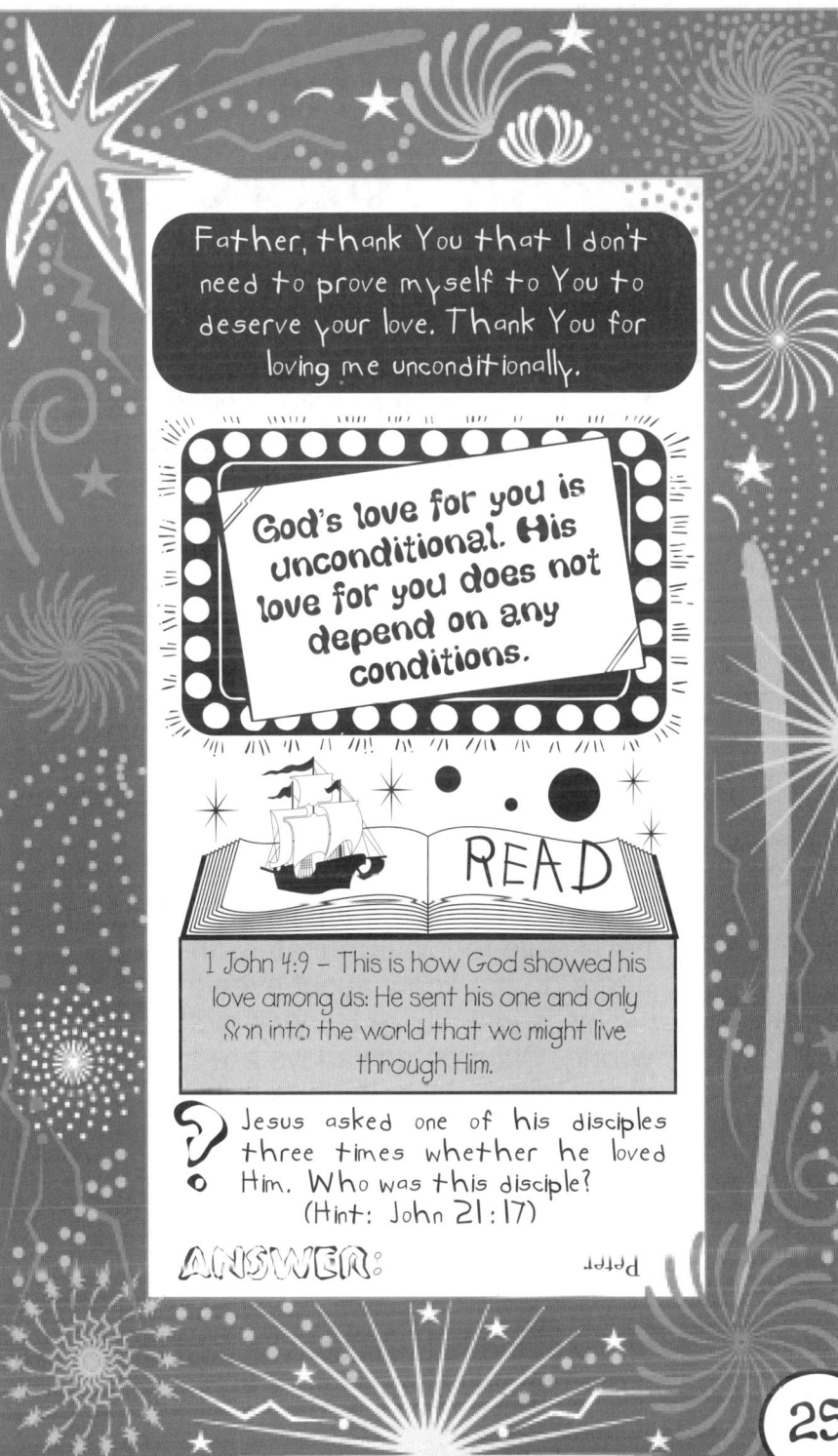

God is holding your future in his hand

Henry was sitting round the corner of the sitting-room eavesdropping, while his parents were having coffee with and talking to their pleasant neighbours.

"Yes," Henry's father was saying, "it is hard to raise children nowadays. One never knows what will become of them." The woman from next door was listening to what Henry's father had to say and in reply told him about her cousin's child who went overseas to look for work because she could not find any in South Africa.

"Yes," Henry's mother replied, "the future is uncertain. I am so glad that I am not a child today. Fortunately, the poor dears do not know about everything."

This is just where Henry's mother was wrong. Children nowadays are aware of many things. Most important, however, is to know that God tells you in Jeremiah 29:11 that He wants you to have plans for the future. This means that He wants you to have hope for the future, because He is your God and your Father who is taking care of you. You need not be afraid of the future, because God is already holding your future in his hand.

Lord, thank You that I may have hope for the future. Thank You that You are completely in control of my future.

God is holding your future in his hand and He wants you to have hope for the future.

READ

Jeremiah 29:11 – "For I know the plans I have for you," declares the Lord, "plans to prosper you and not to harm you, plans to give you hope and a future."

? God promised a well-known man and his wife a son and many descendants. This man and woman were both very old and it seemed as if the promise would never come true. Who were this man and his wife to whom God gave his promise? How old were they?

(Hint: Genesis 17:17)

ANSWER:

Abraham and Sarah, Abraham was 100 and Sarah was 90

Jesus sets you free

Police had been searching for a long time for the cunning thief who, within a week, had broken into four houses in the area where Peter and his folks lived. At last the Friday evening on which the police decided to waylay him, arrived. And, indeed, they caught him while he was trying to break into yet another house. The police questioned him to find out why he broke into people's houses. The handcuffed crook answered that he had thought it would make him rich. He thought he would be free if he could steal other people's belongings to enrich himself.

Many people think that being free means not to have to follow any rules. They think that they can commit sinful deeds without having to bother about God's rules or any other rules. If you also think so, the same thing will happen to you as to the crook: You will end up in the chains of sin and these chains will imprison you. What you thought would set you free, in the end gets a tight hold on you.

The Lord promises in John 8:36 that Jesus can really set you free. You can openly confess your sins to God. Jesus frees you from these sins.

Jesus, thank You for really setting me free from my sins. Thank You that I may confess my sins to You and may know that You will set me free from them.

Jesus really sets you free from all your sins.

READ

Galatians 5:1 – It is for freedom that Christ has set us free.

From which sin in your life do you not yet feel freed? Write it down in the space below and ask Jesus to set you free from it forever.

ANSWER: _____

God also wants you to rest

Lisa was studying very hard for the geography test she was writing the next day. Her mother worried about her, because she hardly ever set foot from her room. All she had been doing the past week was to study and study and study even more. For she was in the middle of the test week.

Lisa was still studying when her mother had to drive her to her music lesson. Lisa didn't want to go, because she didn't have enough time to practice properly. Her mother reminded her to put on her netball clothes, because after her music lesson she had a netball practice and she could not disappoint her team now by not attending the practice. That evening Lisa was tired and tearful. She found everything just too much to handle.

Perhaps you sometimes also feel like this because your programme is too full. God says in Genesis 2:2 that He rested after creating the earth and everything upon it. You also need rest after having worked very hard. Listen to God and see to it that your busy schedule includes enough time to rest and to relax.

Lord, thank You that your Word teaches me to rest sometimes. Please help me to draw up my program in such a way that I get enough rest.

God wants you to rest, even though you have a very full programme.

READ

Genesis 2:3 – And God blessed the seventh day and made it holy, because on it He rested from all the work of creating that He had done.

Write down some of the activities in which you are involved. Think about homework, sport, choir, household chores, playing, etc. Discuss it with your parents if you feel that you have too many activities. Let them help you draw up a plan to make sure that you get enough rest.

God holds you close to his heart

It is always fun to see the first graders run at an athletics meeting. And Christian had trained so hard during their holiday at the seaside. For you see, he was in the big school at last and it was his first athletics meeting. The shot rang out and he was running beautifully. But the next moment he stumbled and fell flat on his tummy. With tears in his eyes he came running to his father. His father picked him up, gave him a big hug and told him how much he loved him. In a short while his tears had dried and he forgot all about his tumble.

God tells you that He is the Shepherd and you are the lamb whom He loves very much. He looks after you. When you have fallen and need to be comforted, He picks you up and holds you close to his heart. You can be sure that your special place with God is close to his heart. Because He thinks you are very special and because He loves you very much, He always carries you there – close to his heart.

God made you for a unique purpose

Derek was feeling unhappy. "Miss Cathy," he asked, "why do you always send Peter to fetch something for you? All I ever have to do, is to sweep the classroom. You always give Peter the most important job."

"Derek, I always send Peter because he finishes his work quickly. I always ask you to clean the classroom because you do it so well. Both these jobs are important to me. We can't all be sent on errands or asked to clean the classroom."

God made each person for a very specific purpose. God likes to use you and you must serve Him with all your heart. In God's hand you are a tool with a specific purpose. Isaiah 64:8 says you are like clay in his hands. He created you and forms you for a specific purpose.

In the kitchen there are various containers: cups, bowls, pots and pans. Every container has a purpose, a reason why it was made. And it is supposed to be used for that purpose. We are also like the containers in a kitchen. And God has a very special task for each of us.

You are a winner

James was talking to Gerald, his elder brother. "You are a winner – a champ. When you run, you come first. You play for the first rugby team. And you always have the highest marks in class."

"I think you are a winner too," Gerald answered.

"You must be joking, man. I just manage to scrape through to the next grade. I can't run very fast and I play for the C team."

"James, I know that you have given your life to Jesus. So you are in God's team and his team is always the winning team. Only those people who are in the winning team will get into heaven one day. That is why you are a winner."

Jesus said that there is room enough in his Father's house for all who love Him. John 14:2 says Jesus went to heaven to prepare a place for us, and someday Jesus will return to fetch his winning team to live with Him forever.

When you choose to be on the side of Jesus, you are in the winning team. And when you have God on your side, no-one can be against you.

Lord, thank you that I may be in your winning team.

When you have given your life to the Lord, you are in the winning team and will one day live with Him in heaven.

READ

Romans 8:37 — No, in all these things we are more than conquerors through him who loved us.

In Samuel 17 we read about someone who was in the winning team. He told his opponent, "You come against me with sword and spear and javelin, but I come against you in the name of the Lord Almighty." Who was this winner?

(Hint: 1 Samuel 17:45)

ANSWER: David

8

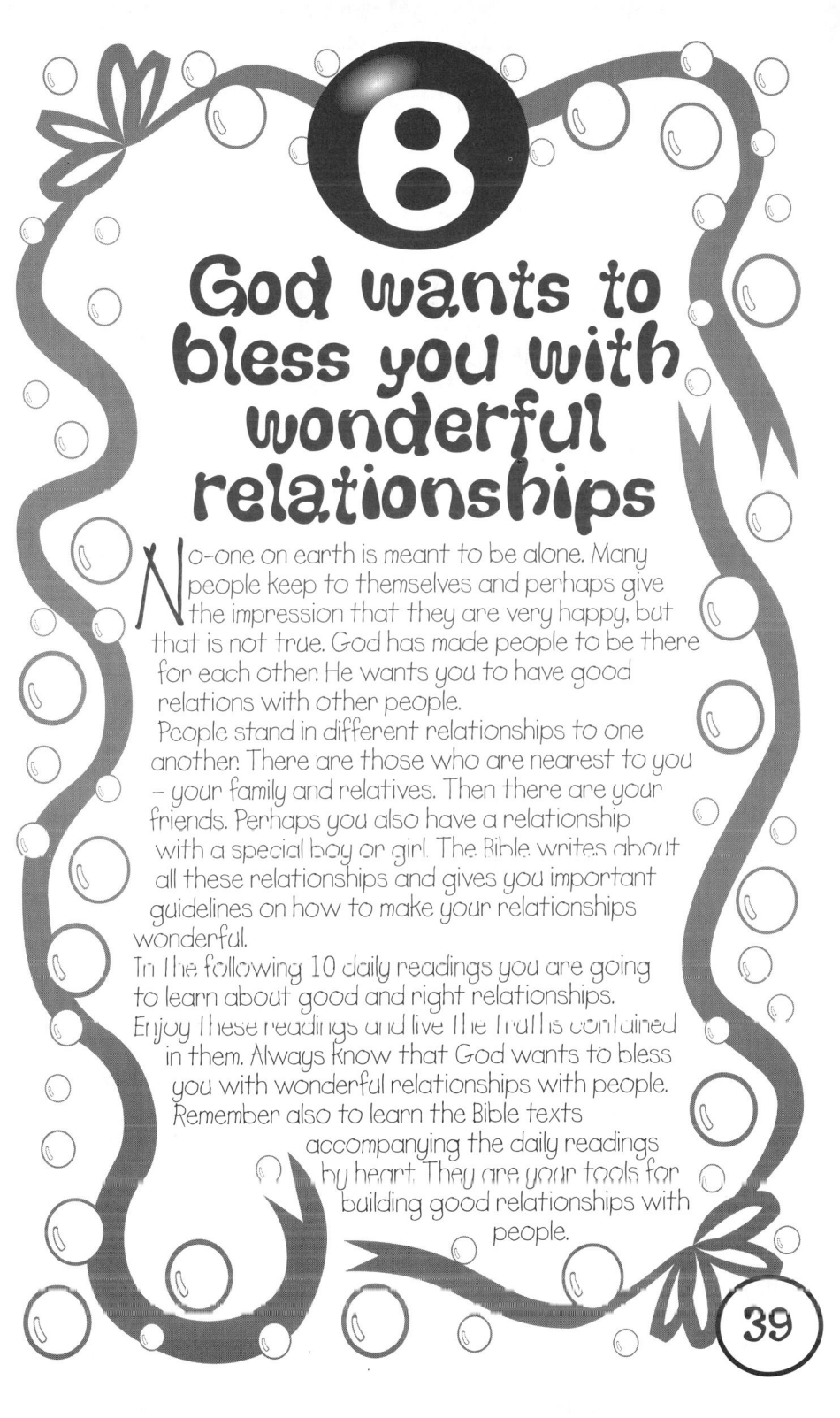

God wants to bless you with wonderful relationships

No-one on earth is meant to be alone. Many people keep to themselves and perhaps give the impression that they are very happy, but that is not true. God has made people to be there for each other. He wants you to have good relations with other people.

People stand in different relationships to one another. There are those who are nearest to you – your family and relatives. Then there are your friends. Perhaps you also have a relationship with a special boy or girl. The Bible writes about all these relationships and gives you important guidelines on how to make your relationships wonderful.

In the following 10 daily readings you are going to learn about good and right relationships. Enjoy these readings and live the truths contained in them. Always know that God wants to bless you with wonderful relationships with people. Remember also to learn the Bible texts accompanying the daily readings by heart. They are your tools for building good relationships with people.

God wants you to honour your parents

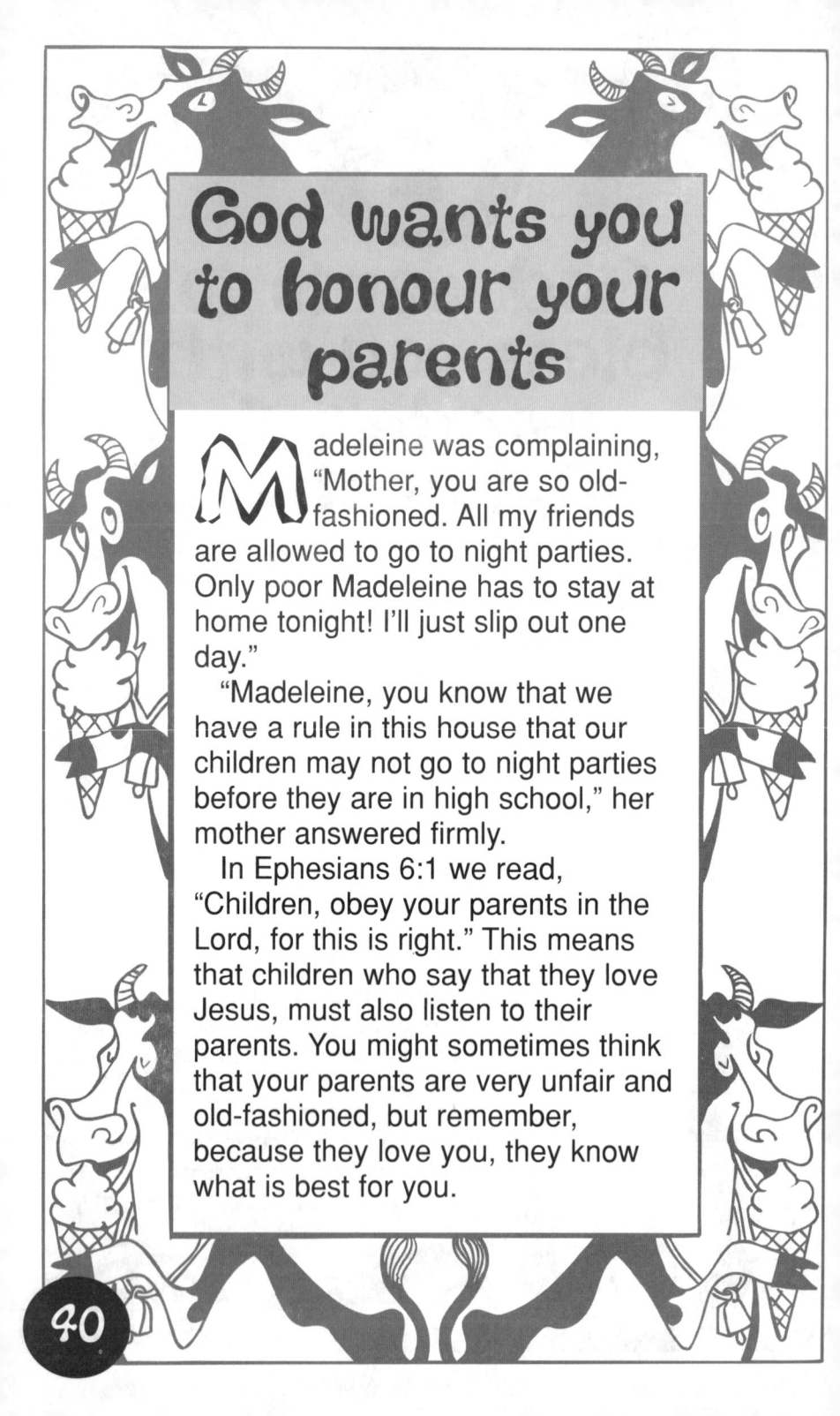

Madeleine was complaining, "Mother, you are so old-fashioned. All my friends are allowed to go to night parties. Only poor Madeleine has to stay at home tonight! I'll just slip out one day."

"Madeleine, you know that we have a rule in this house that our children may not go to night parties before they are in high school," her mother answered firmly.

In Ephesians 6:1 we read, "Children, obey your parents in the Lord, for this is right." This means that children who say that they love Jesus, must also listen to their parents. You might sometimes think that your parents are very unfair and old-fashioned, but remember, because they love you, they know what is best for you.

Do you think it would be fun to live in a home where there are no rules? Certainly not! Think about the chaos of untidy rooms and homework that is never done. Your parents' discipline shows very clearly that they care a lot about you. And because you are precious to God, He has given you to parents who love you and help you do the right thing.

Children who love God, also listen to their parents.

Lord, thank You very much for my parents. Please help me to be an obedient child.

READ

Colossians 3:20 – Children, obey your parents in everything, for this pleases the Lord.

How old was Adam when his son Seth was born?

(Hint: Genesis 5:3)

ANSWER: 130

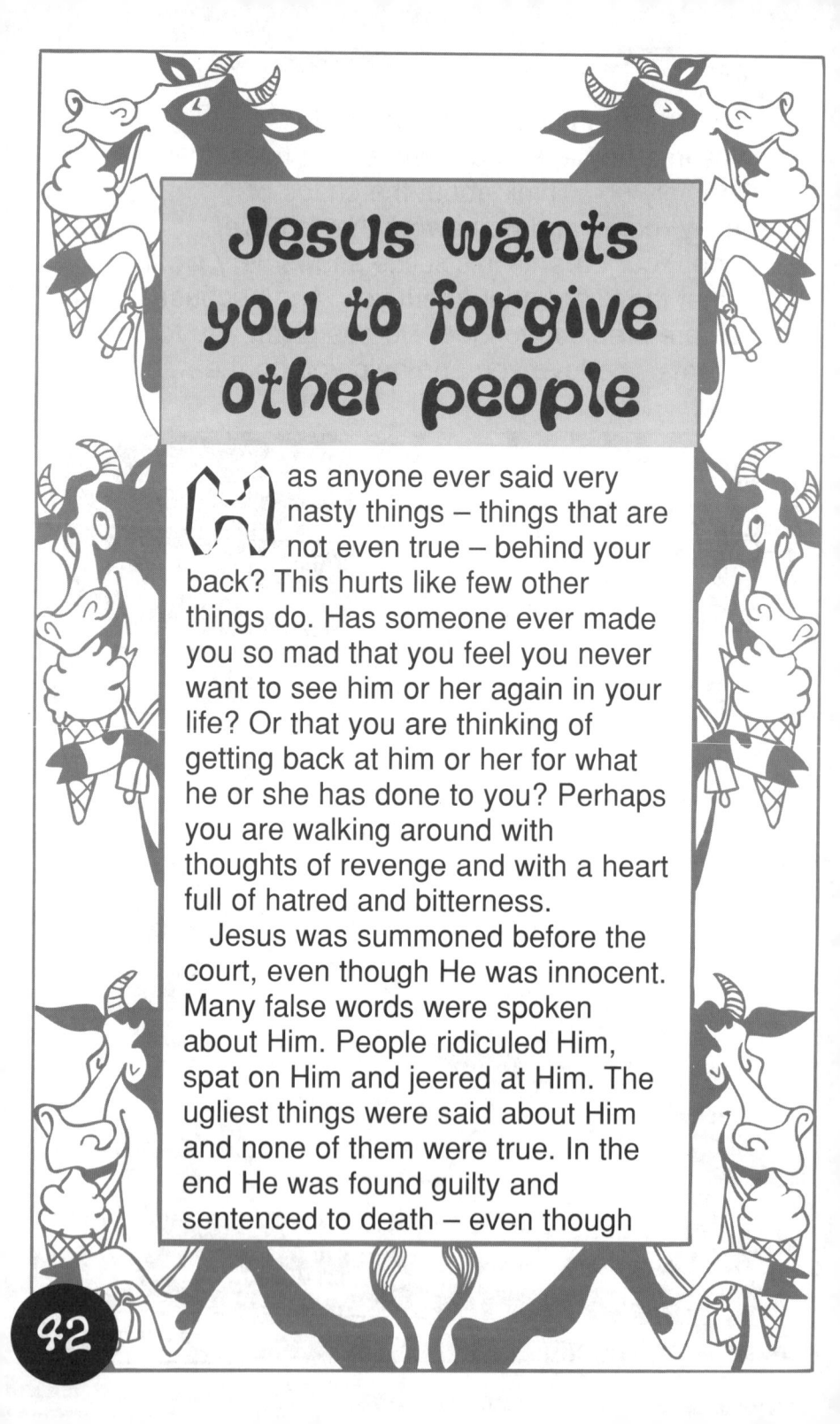

Jesus wants you to forgive other people

Has anyone ever said very nasty things – things that are not even true – behind your back? This hurts like few other things do. Has someone ever made you so mad that you feel you never want to see him or her again in your life? Or that you are thinking of getting back at him or her for what he or she has done to you? Perhaps you are walking around with thoughts of revenge and with a heart full of hatred and bitterness.

Jesus was summoned before the court, even though He was innocent. Many false words were spoken about Him. People ridiculed Him, spat on Him and jeered at Him. The ugliest things were said about Him and none of them were true. In the end He was found guilty and sentenced to death – even though

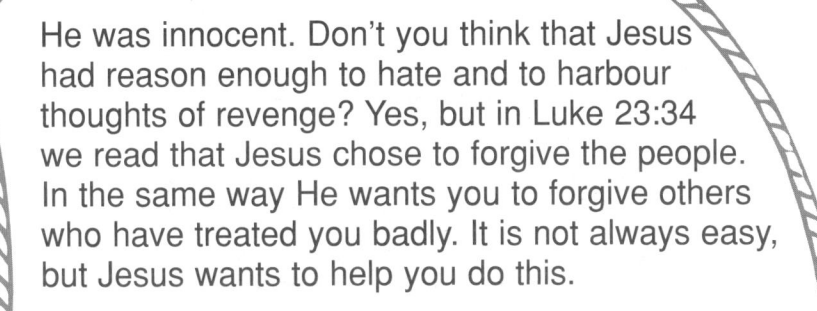

He was innocent. Don't you think that Jesus had reason enough to hate and to harbour thoughts of revenge? Yes, but in Luke 23:34 we read that Jesus chose to forgive the people. In the same way He wants you to forgive others who have treated you badly. It is not always easy, but Jesus wants to help you do this.

> You can forgive those people who have hurt you.

> Jesus, today I choose to forgive the people who have treated me badly and who have hurt me. Please help me each day to choose to forgive others.

READ

Luke 11:4 – Forgive us our sins, for we also forgive everyone who sins against us.

Who forgave his brothers after they had hurt him very much and treated him badly?

(Hint: Genesis 45 : 4-5)

ANSWER: Joseph

God wants you to choose your friends carefully

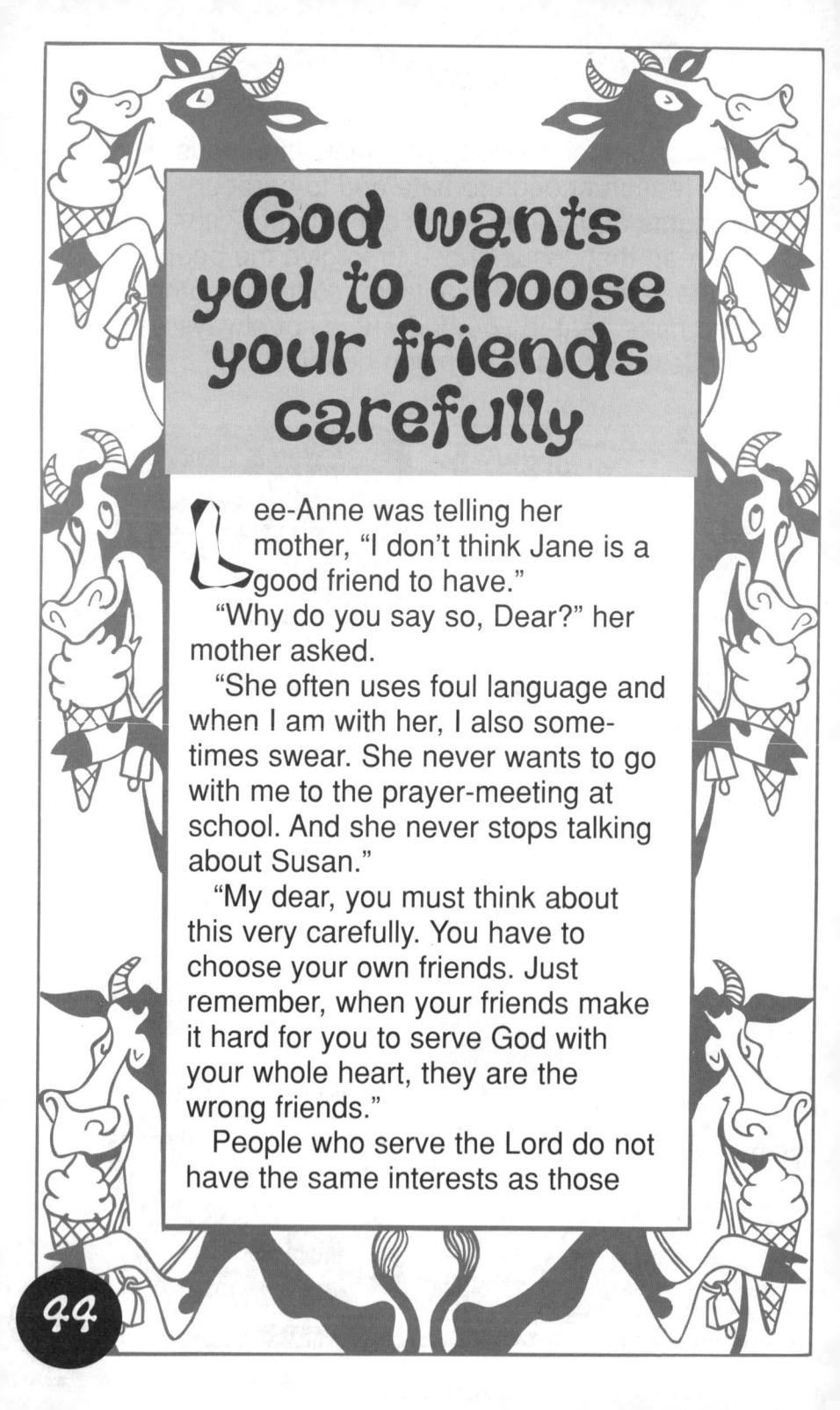

Lee-Anne was telling her mother, "I don't think Jane is a good friend to have."

"Why do you say so, Dear?" her mother asked.

"She often uses foul language and when I am with her, I also sometimes swear. She never wants to go with me to the prayer-meeting at school. And she never stops talking about Susan."

"My dear, you must think about this very carefully. You have to choose your own friends. Just remember, when your friends make it hard for you to serve God with your whole heart, they are the wrong friends."

People who serve the Lord do not have the same interests as those who don't serve Him. When you love God, you like to talk about Him. You can't share your heart's secrets with someone who doesn't serve Jesus. Remember: birds of a feather flock together. In Proverbs 18:24 the Bible specifically warns against friends who can ruin you. This means that they can lead you astray – on a road away from God.

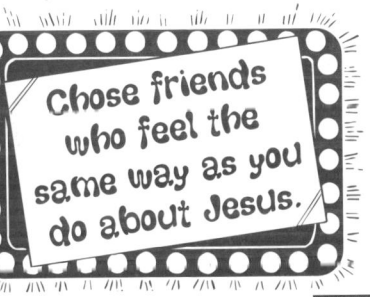

Chose friends who feel the same way as you do about Jesus.

Lord, You want me to have good friends. Help me to make the correct choices when I choose them.

READ

2 Corinthians 6:14 – Do not be yoked together with unbelievers.

? Daniel had good friends who also served the Lord. What were their names?

(Hint: Daniel 2:17)

ANSWER: Hananiah, Mishael and Azariah. They were also called Shadrach, Meshach and Abednego

45

God wants you to have good friends

William, or rather Wild William, slipped while he was climbing a mountain. They rushed him to hospital, where they found his arm had two bad fractures. They had to operate. William, who was always full of fun and on the go, did not like the idea of staying in hospital. But then one day two of his friends surprised him by visiting him in hospital. They brought sweets, cool drink and a lovely board game with them. The three laughed and played and in a short time the afternoon passed. William was sorry to see them go. He said goodbye to them with the words, "Thank you. You are true friends."

A true friend is someone who stands by you through thick and thin. Even when things go wrong, a true friend will always be there for you. It is someone who serves Jesus like you do. In Proverbs 17:17 the Bible says that you can always rely on such a friend's love and that he or she will always be there for you, even in times of distress.

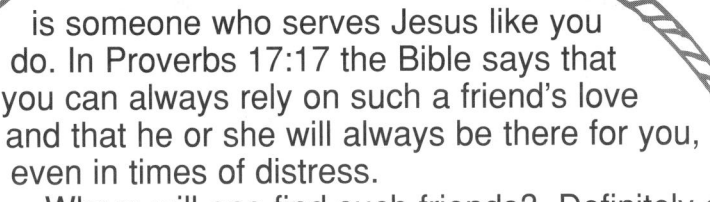

Where will one find such friends? Definitely at the church, the SU and other spiritual gatherings. Try to find such friends, because God wants to give you good friends like these.

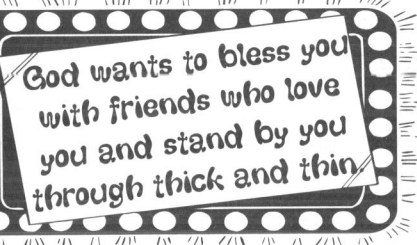

God wants to bless you with friends who love you and stand by you through thick and thin.

Lord, please help me to look for and to find friends who also love You and who will stand by me through thick and thin.

READ

Proverbs 17:17 – A friend loves at all times, and a brother is born for adversity.

Who in the Bible were bosom friends and an example of true friendship?

(Hint: 1 Samuel 23:18)

ANSWER: David and Jonathan

47

Your family is precious to God

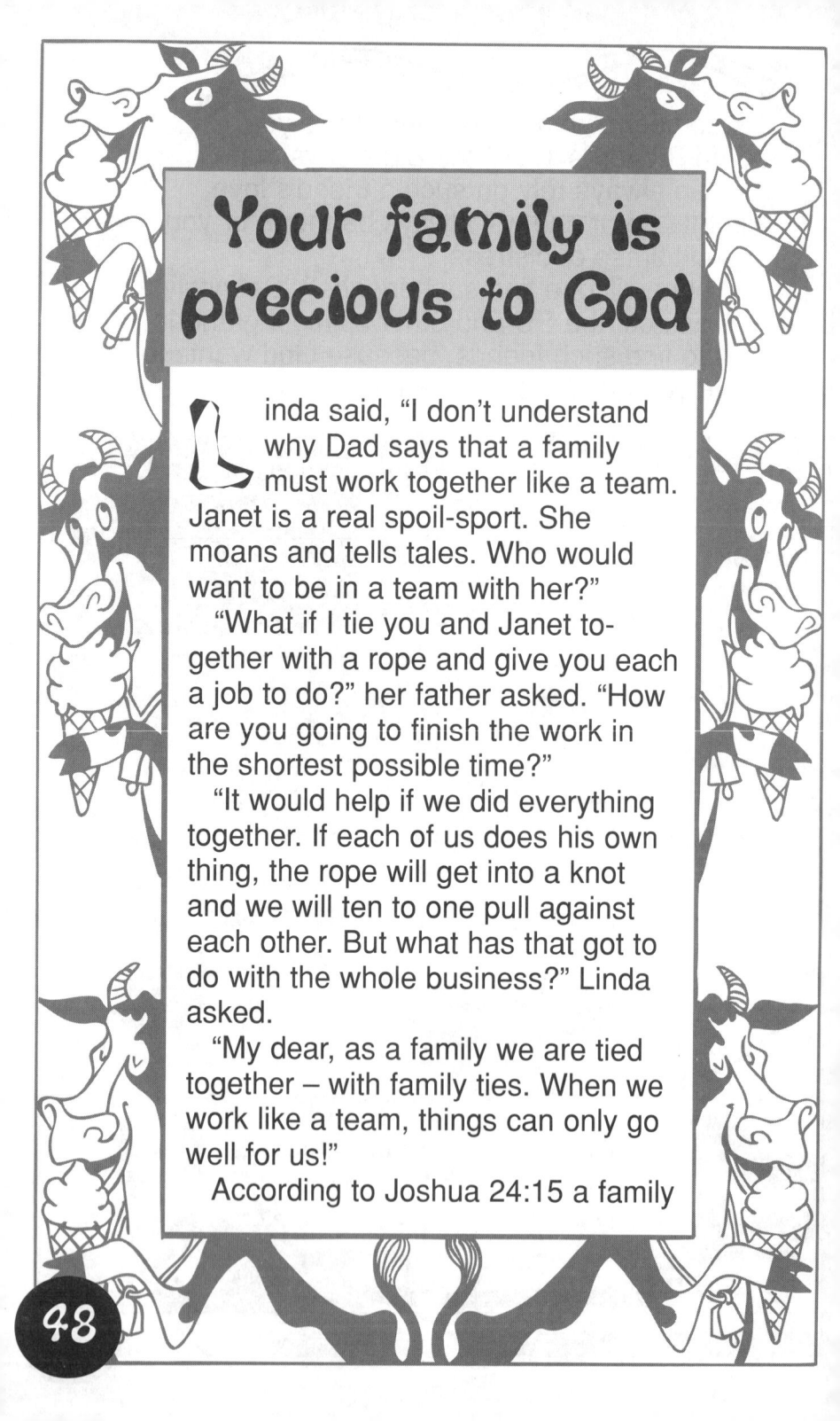

Linda said, "I don't understand why Dad says that a family must work together like a team. Janet is a real spoil-sport. She moans and tells tales. Who would want to be in a team with her?"

"What if I tie you and Janet together with a rope and give you each a job to do?" her father asked. "How are you going to finish the work in the shortest possible time?"

"It would help if we did everything together. If each of us does his own thing, the rope will get into a knot and we will ten to one pull against each other. But what has that got to do with the whole business?" Linda asked.

"My dear, as a family we are tied together – with family ties. When we work like a team, things can only go well for us!"

According to Joshua 24:15 a family

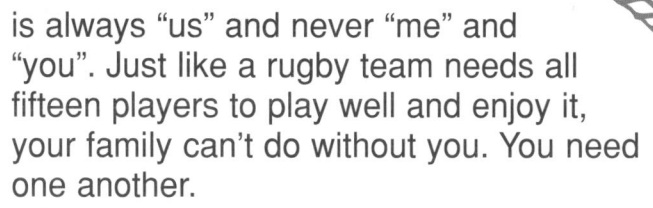

is always "us" and never "me" and "you". Just like a rugby team needs all fifteen players to play well and enjoy it, your family can't do without you. You need one another.

Have you ever told your brothers and sisters that they are precious to you? Do you treat them as if they are valuable to you and also to God?

A family works together as a team.

Lord, thank You very much for giving me a family. Please help us to work together as a team.

READ

Joshua 24:15 – But as for me and my household, we will serve the Lord.

What were the names of Jesus' brothers?

(Hint: Mark 6:3)

ANSWER:

James, Joseph, Judas and Simon

You can help others

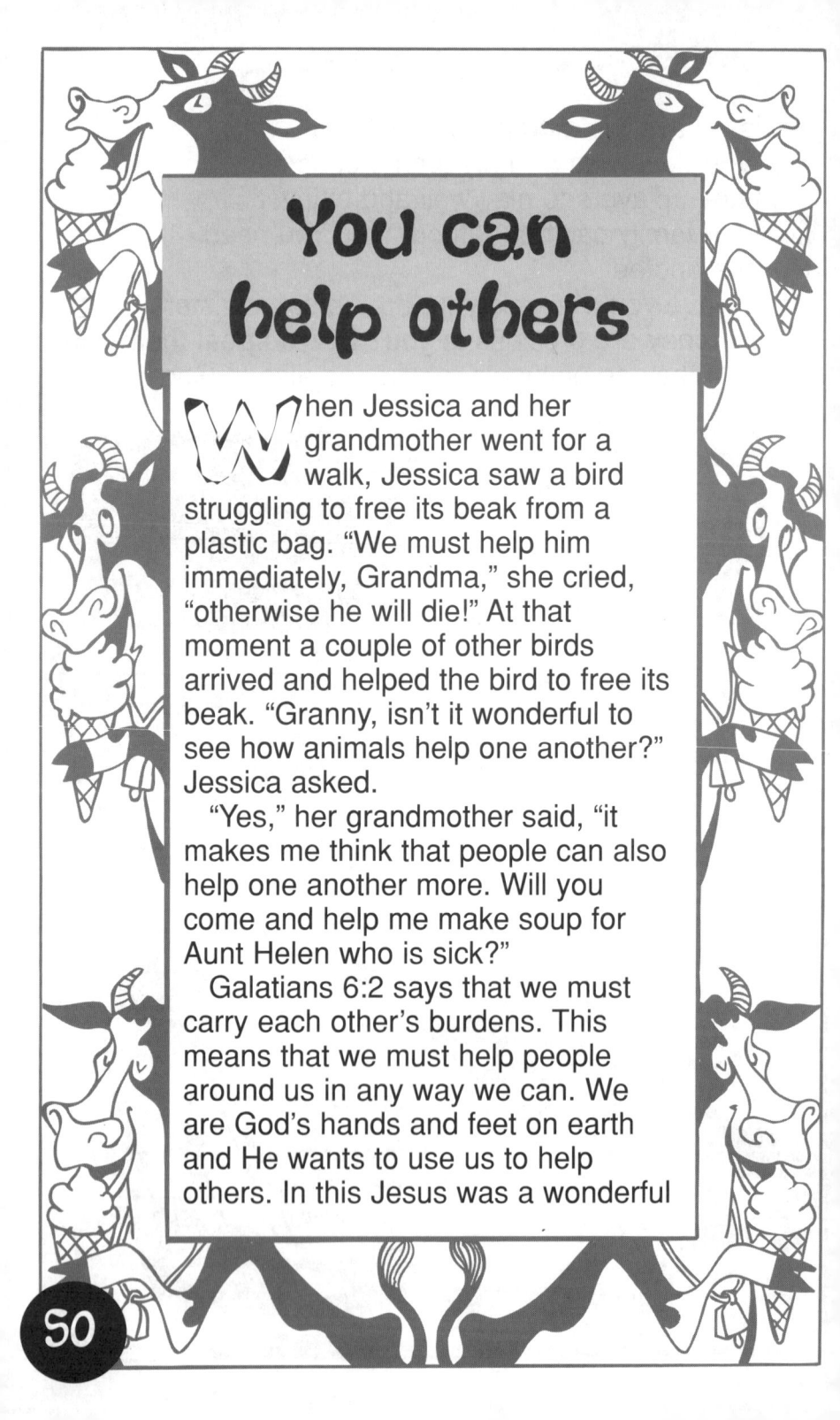

When Jessica and her grandmother went for a walk, Jessica saw a bird struggling to free its beak from a plastic bag. "We must help him immediately, Grandma," she cried, "otherwise he will die!" At that moment a couple of other birds arrived and helped the bird to free its beak. "Granny, isn't it wonderful to see how animals help one another?" Jessica asked.

"Yes," her grandmother said, "it makes me think that people can also help one another more. Will you come and help me make soup for Aunt Helen who is sick?"

Galatians 6:2 says that we must carry each other's burdens. This means that we must help people around us in any way we can. We are God's hands and feet on earth and He wants to use us to help others. In this Jesus was a wonderful example. He helped people wherever He went. What can you do?

- You can share your food during break with those who didn't bring anything.
- You can help your mother in the house when you see that she is tired.
- You can invite the child who has no friends to come and play with you and your friends.

God wants you to become aware of other people's burdens and to make them lighter by helping to carry them.

Lord, help me to see other people's needs and to help them wherever I can.

READ

Galatians 6:9 – Let us not become weary in doing good.

Which parable tells us about a man who carried someone else's burdens?

(Hint: Luke 10 : 25-37)

ANSWER:

The parable of the good Samaritan

You can be a good friend

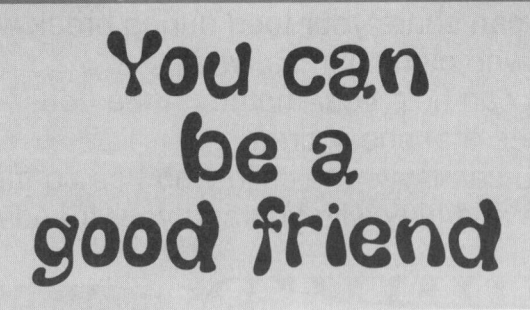

Janet and her mother were busy washing up after supper.

"Mum, today in the PT class I was so glad that Judy is my friend," Janet said. "A group of girls laughed at me and teased me because I still couldn't get the dance steps right. Judy then said that they could laugh, but that I am her friend and I have many good qualities."

Her mother hung up the dishcloth. "My dear, now you know that Judy is a true friend. She could have laughed at you too, but she was loyal to you. In Proverbs we read a lot about friendship. And Proverbs 17:17 says, 'A friend loves at all times.' I know that you always will be a good friend to Judy too."

In Proverbs 18:24 we read that friends can be closer to one than a brother (or a sister). And isn't it wonderful to know that Jesus wants to be our best friend? Are you a friend that builds up or breaks down?

> Try your best to always be a friend who will build up others.

> Lord, please help me to always be a friend who builds up. Forgive me for those times when I was a friend who broke down.

READ

Proverbs 18:24 – A man of many companions may come to ruin, but there is a friend who sticks closer than a brother.

At your school there will surely be children who do not have friends. You can be a special friend to them. Invite them during break to come and talk to you and your friends and to play with you.

Your parents can also make mistakes

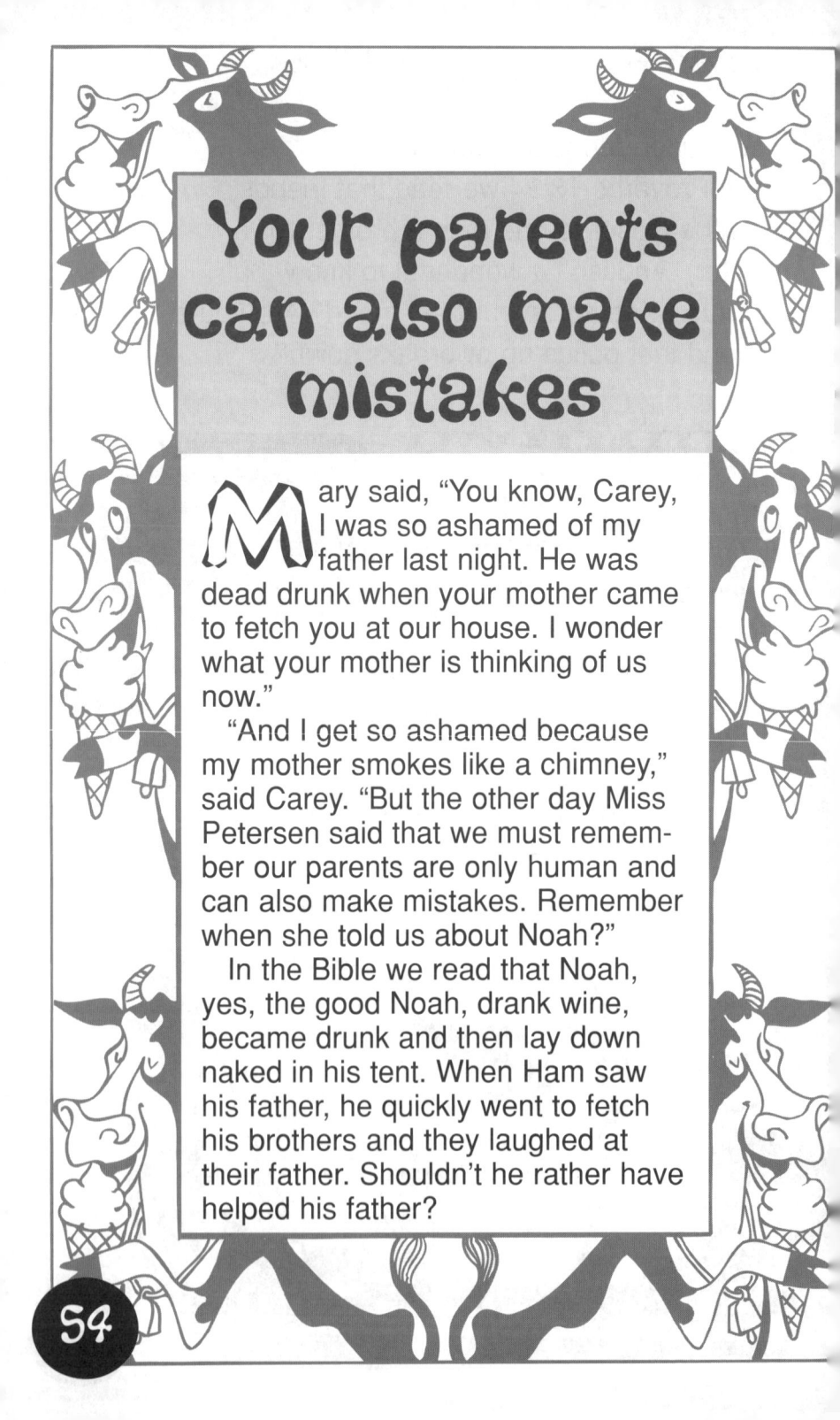

Mary said, "You know, Carey, I was so ashamed of my father last night. He was dead drunk when your mother came to fetch you at our house. I wonder what your mother is thinking of us now."

"And I get so ashamed because my mother smokes like a chimney," said Carey. "But the other day Miss Petersen said that we must remember our parents are only human and can also make mistakes. Remember when she told us about Noah?"

In the Bible we read that Noah, yes, the good Noah, drank wine, became drunk and then lay down naked in his tent. When Ham saw his father, he quickly went to fetch his brothers and they laughed at their father. Shouldn't he rather have helped his father?

Even Christian parents sometimes do things that shame their children. If you say that you have given your life to the Lord, you must treat your parents the way God expects you to – with respect. Your father and mother are still your parents and also people who are precious to God, even though they sometimes make mistakes.

God wants you to always treat your parents with respect, even though they sometimes do things that make you ashamed.

Lord, please help me to always treat my parents with respect, even though they sometimes make mistakes.

READ

Exodus 20:12 – Honour your father and your mother, so that you may live long in the land the Lord your God is giving you.

What did Noah's two other sons, Shem and Japheth, do when they saw their father naked? (Hint: Genesis 9:23)

ANSWER: They covered him with his clothes

55

God will bless you in his own time with a special friend - boy or girl

Sheila and Frank were only in grade 7, but they spent all their time in each other's company. Frank's friends didn't like the idea that their friend never spent time with them any more. Sheila's friends were mad at her, because she was spending all her time with Frank. It seemed as if they were not important to Sheila any more.

Do you think it is a good thing to spend all your time with one person when you are still so young? You are missing out on much fun with the rest of your friends. They are doing interesting things and enjoying each other's company – while you and that one person are cooing in each other's ears all the time.

God wants to bless you with many

friends now and later on with someone with whom you can share the rest of your life. In Ecclesiastes 4:9-10 God says that a group of friends can help one another in wonderful ways. A group of friends can help you get up when you have fallen and be there for you when things are not going well.

One day God will bless you with a special boyfriend or girlfriend. Now is the time to enjoy the company of a group of friends.

Lord, please help me to recognise the value of a big circle of friends. Please help me not to commit myself to a relationship with just one person.

READ

Ecclesiastes 4:12 – Though one may be overpowered, two can defend themselves. A cord of three strands is not quickly broken.

Fill in the missing words of this Bible text:
Perfume and _____ bring joy to the heart, but the pleasantness of _____ springs from his _____
Proverbs 27:9

God gives us sex, but it can also be dangerous

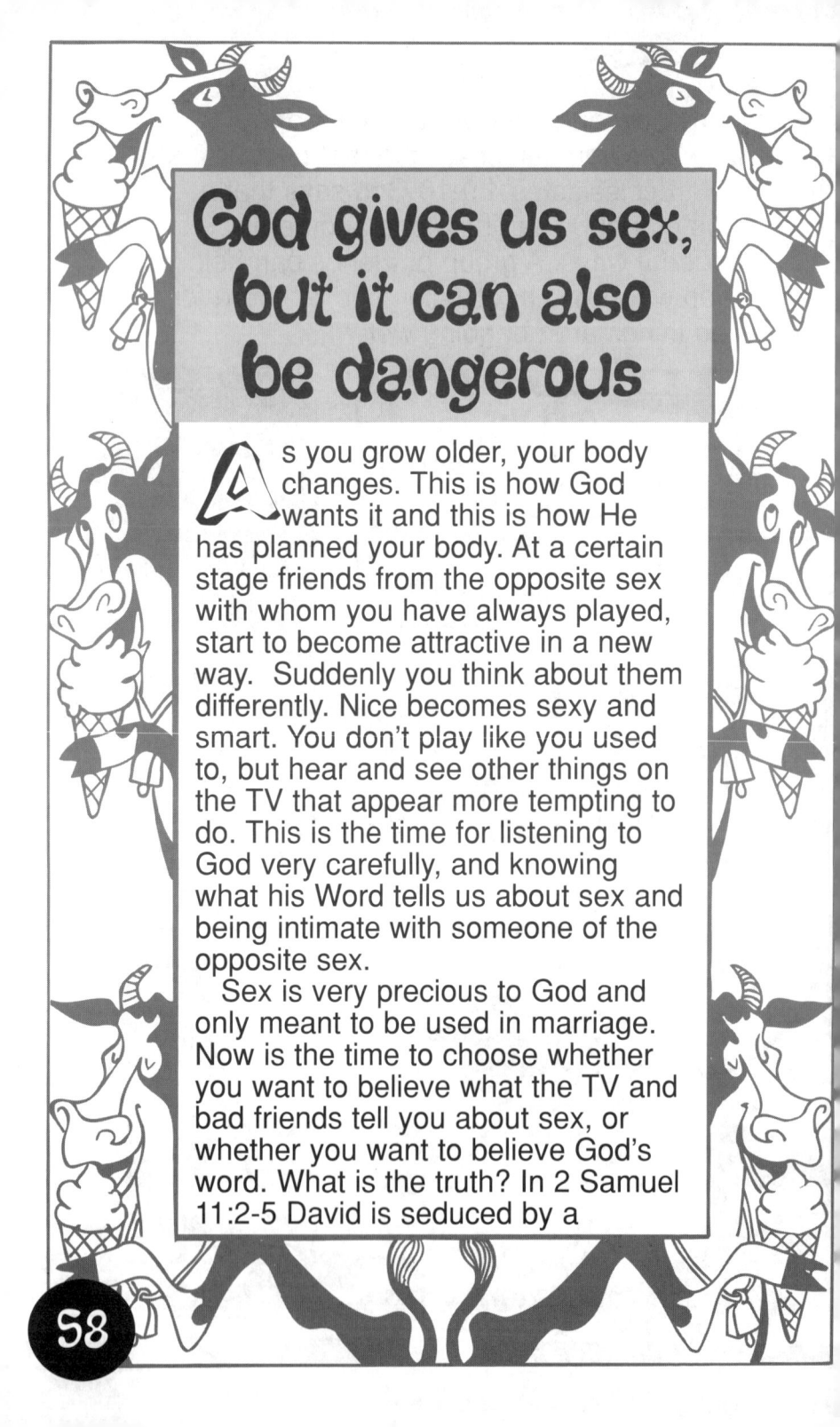

As you grow older, your body changes. This is how God wants it and this is how He has planned your body. At a certain stage friends from the opposite sex with whom you have always played, start to become attractive in a new way. Suddenly you think about them differently. Nice becomes sexy and smart. You don't play like you used to, but hear and see other things on the TV that appear more tempting to do. This is the time for listening to God very carefully, and knowing what his Word tells us about sex and being intimate with someone of the opposite sex.

Sex is very precious to God and only meant to be used in marriage. Now is the time to choose whether you want to believe what the TV and bad friends tell you about sex, or whether you want to believe God's word. What is the truth? In 2 Samuel 11:2-5 David is seduced by a beautiful married woman. He doesn't listen to God and goes to bed with her. Afterwards he hears that she is pregnant. He then kills her husband in order to marry her. Not listening to what God says on sexual matters always has unpleasant results. Choose now whether you want to save your body for one day when God will give you the right husband or wife.

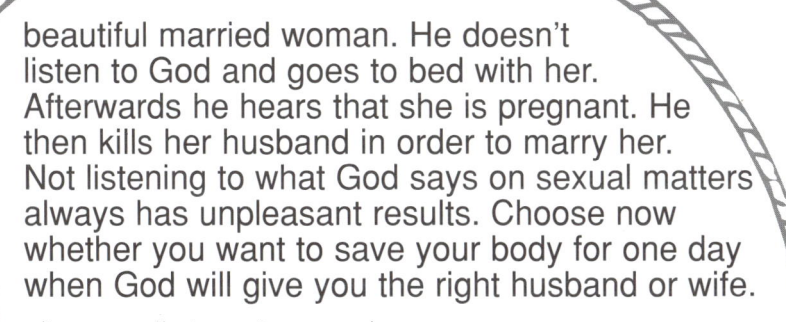

> God created sex for a man and a woman to enjoy when they are married.

> Lord, I choose to save my body for the husband or wife You are going to give to me. Please help me always to remember it, especially in times when someone wants to abuse me.

READ

Proverbs 6:32 – But a man who commits adultery lacks judgment; whoever does so destroys himself.

Who is the young man who fled from a sexual temptation because he wanted to stay faithful to God?

(Hint: Genesis 39 : 12)

ANSWER: Joseph

God is always with you

It is impossible to have someone special with you all the time. Your father or mother can't go to school with you, your best friend can't play with you all day and your grandmother and grandfather might live in another town. But here's the good news! God is always with you – that same God who loves you so much.

Whether you are sleeping, playing, taking part in sport or studying for a test – God is with you. You can trust Him with everything in your life. You can tell Him everything that is happening to you – good or bad. He is with you everywhere and always.

In the following 7 daily readings you are going to hear more about this God to whom you are so precious that He is always with you. Remember to read the Bible texts until you know them by heart, because the Word of God is the truth and truth chases untruth away.

God takes care of you

Gerald loved animals. One evening he was watching one of his favourite nature programmes on TV. He saw how a woman was feeding three baby birds with a medicine dropper. Their little beaks were wide open and he heard them chirping for food. Gerald was quite worried and asked his mother, "Where is the mother of the chicks? Isn't she supposed to feed them?" His mother explained that some birds kick their young out of the nest or just fly away and leave them on their own.

There is one thing you can be sure of: God will never do to his children what some bird mothers do to theirs. In Matthew 6:26 the Lord says that we need not worry, He will take care of us. God is always there and He takes care of you day and night. He will never leave you. He also does not expect you to look after yourself. No, He takes care of us. It is He who gives you food to eat and clothes to wear. So you need never be worried.

> Lord, thank You for looking after me every day. Thank You that I need not worry about food, clothes or anything else.

God takes care of you all the time.

READ

Psalm 37:5 – Commit your way to the Lord; trust in Him and He will do this.

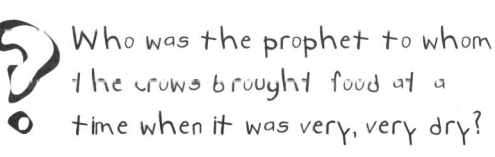

? Who was the prophet to whom the crows brought food at a time when it was very, very dry?

(Hint: 1 Kings 17:2-4)

ANSWER: Elijah

God is always with you

Peter's father had been transferred again. So he was starting his new school year in yet another school. It felt strange each time and he didn't like it at all. He wished that the company his father was working for, would stop transferring him like this.

Peter was sitting in class looking around him. He was feeling very small and lonely. He didn't know anyone. Everything around him was strange and new. Yes, although there were many people around him, he was feeling lonely.

Perhaps you have also felt like this at some time or another. Whether it is a new school, a new class or your parents' new friends, you feel strange and very lonely at first. Worst of all is when you lose your way in a big supermarket and start feeling scared on your own.

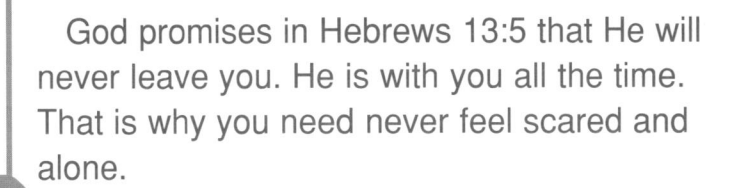

God promises in Hebrews 13:5 that He will never leave you. He is with you all the time. That is why you need never feel scared and alone.

> Lord, thank You that You are with me all the time. Thank You that I am never alone.

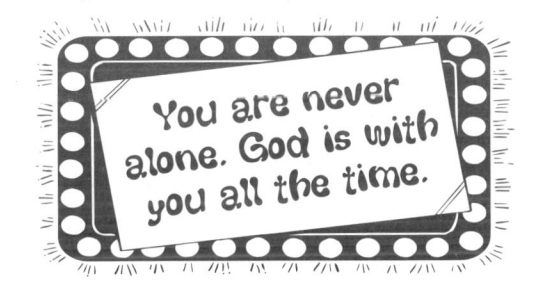

You are never alone. God is with you all the time.

READ

Joshua 1:9 – Do not be terrified; do not be discouraged, for the Lord your God will be with you wherever you go.

? Who was very scared when he heard that a whole crowd of enemies were advancing to make war on the Judeans? (Hint: 2 Chronicles 20 : 2-3)

ANSWER: Jehoshaphat

You need never be afraid

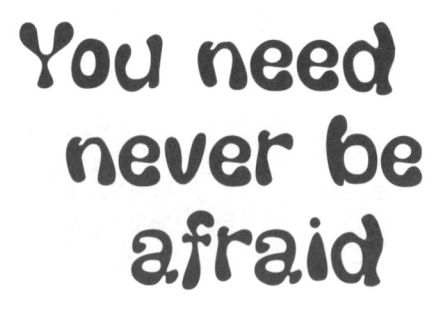

A few friends were having fun playing hide and seek. They hid behind the curtains, under the beds, in the cupboards, and wherever there was a hiding-place. The next moment they heard a frightened, shaky little voice, "I am scared. Please put on the lights." It was Mary. She had become scared in the dark. So she gave away her hiding-place.

Perhaps you are scared of the dark, of fierce dogs or of a strict teacher at school. The Lord tells you in Psalm 27:1 that He is your light and your salvation. You need not be scared of anything or anyone. The Lord doesn't want you to go through life with fear in your heart. He protects you. So you need never be afraid. You can be sure that God is with you all the time and that He is taking care of you.

> Lord, thank You that You are my light and my salvation and that I need never be afraid.

The Lord protects you. You need never be afraid.

READ

Psalm 27:1 – The Lord is my light and my salvation – whom shall I fear?

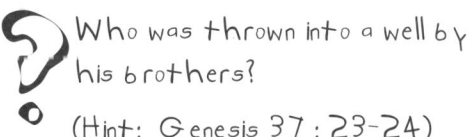

? Who was thrown into a well by his brothers?

(Hint: Genesis 37 : 23-24)

ANSWER: Joseph

You belong to the King

King Edward VII was one of the kings of England. He had a dog named Caesar. He and Caesar loved each other very much. Everywhere the king went, Caesar went. In the palace the dog always sat at the king's feet.

One day the king thought of a clever plan. He was afraid that Caesar would get lost and that the person who found him, wouldn't know whose dog it was. The king then had a collar made with the following words on it, "I belong to the king" and put it around Caesar's neck.

When the king died, Caesar also attended the funeral. With his tail between his legs he followed the funeral procession. He was faithful to his master until death.

In Revelation 11:15 we read that God will be King for ever and ever. We know that God the King is also our Father. As children of God, we need not wear collars. People should be able to see that we belong to the King and love Him by the way we are living.

> Lord, thanks that I may belong to You, the only King. Please help me to live like a King's child all the time.

You belong to the King of kings.

READ

Psalm 145:1 – I will exalt You, my God the King; I will praise your Name for ever and ever.

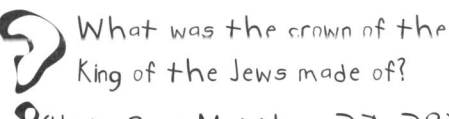

? What was the crown of the King of the Jews made of?
(Hint: Read Matthew 27:29)

ANSWER: Thorn-tree branches

God holds your hand tightly

Have you ever walked in the veld on a farm after dark? It usually is so dark that you can't see your hand in front of your eyes. This is exactly what happened to Jerry and Abe. They went camping with their fathers and in the evening the two of them went for a walk. Suddenly they realised that they were lost. They had no idea in which direction the tent was and they couldn't see a thing. They were very scared and started calling their fathers. The next moment they saw the two tiny lights made by their fathers' torches coming their way. Abe and Jerry were very glad. With their hands held tightly in their fathers' hands, they returned to their tents.

Sometimes you also get scared of things that happen in your life. Perhaps you are afraid when you are alone in the dark. Perhaps you are afraid of staying at home alone. In times like these God wants you to ask

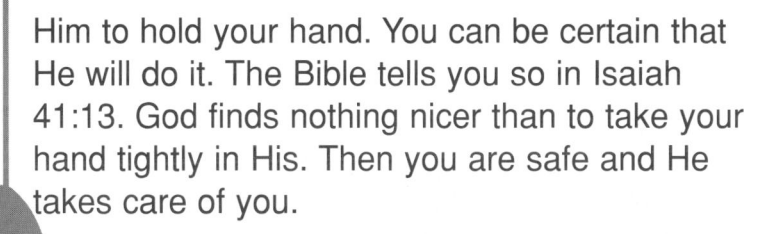

Him to hold your hand. You can be certain that He will do it. The Bible tells you so in Isaiah 41:13. God finds nothing nicer than to take your hand tightly in His. Then you are safe and He takes care of you.

> Lord, thank You for taking my hand in Yours. Thank You that I am safe with You.

God always and in all circumstances holds your hand tightly in His.

READ

Isaiah 41:13 – For I am the Lord, your God, who takes hold of your right hand and says to you, Do not fear; I will help you.

? Who states clearly that he doesn't run away when he is afraid, but takes refuge in God?
(Hint: Psalm 11:1)

ANSWER: David

God always listens to you

Ryan is very unhappy. Last night, when his father came home, he was eager to tell him about the rugby match he had played. But guests arrived and his father just said, "Children must be seen and not heard." So Ryan sat all by himself all evening. The quests went home after he had gone to bed.

This morning his father was in a hurry to get to work and Ryan again could not tell him about the match. Ryan was sad, because he thought his father wouldn't listen to him because he didn't care about him. He wanted to talk to his father very much.

The good news is: God is always there when you want to talk to Him. You are so precious to God that you can talk to Him at any time and anywhere. Whether it is on your bike, in class or on the playground – you can talk to God. Philippians 4:6 says that you can tell God about all the things you desire. Best of all is that God wants you to talk to Him. He likes it when you talk to Him. He hears all your prayers.

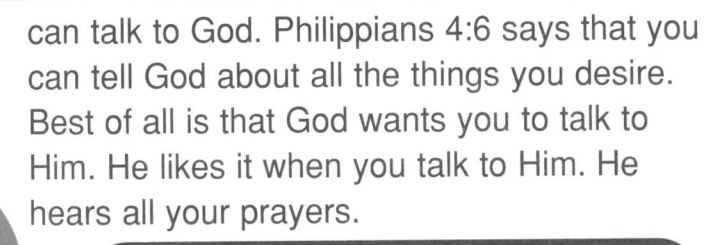

> Father, thank You that You always listen when I speak. Thank You for never being too busy to listen to me.

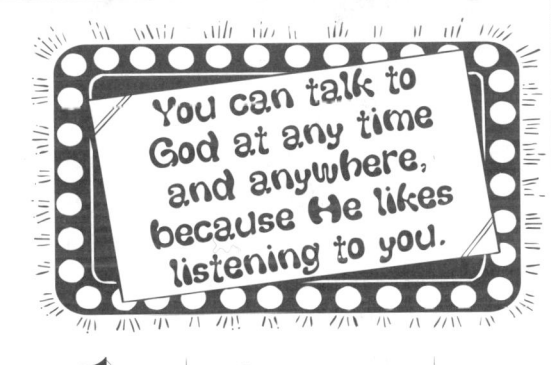

You can talk to God at any time and anywhere, because He likes listening to you.

READ

Philippians 4:6 – Do not be anxious about anything, but in everything, by prayer and petition, with thanksgiving, present your requests to God.

? Who prayed to God before all the prophets of Baal?
(Hint: 1 Kings 18:36)

ANSWER: Elijah

Emmanuel: God is with you

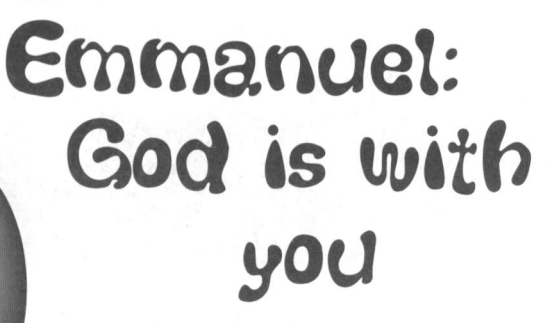

One day a kudu calf strayed from the herd because it was inquisitive. While it was wandering about on its own, a young lion started stalking it. Fortunately the kudu herd realised that the calf was in danger and two of the kudu bulls chased off the lion with their horns.

I can just imagine how scared the little kudu must have been when it saw the lion. It had reason to be afraid, because it was alone. If you know Jesus, you need never feel alone. One of Jesus' names is Emmanuel. In Matthew 1:23 we read what the name Emmanuel means: God with us. When your friends treat you badly because you don't want to do something wrong with them, remember: You are not alone. God is with you. Even if you are not part of the in-group at school, remember: You are not alone. God is with you.

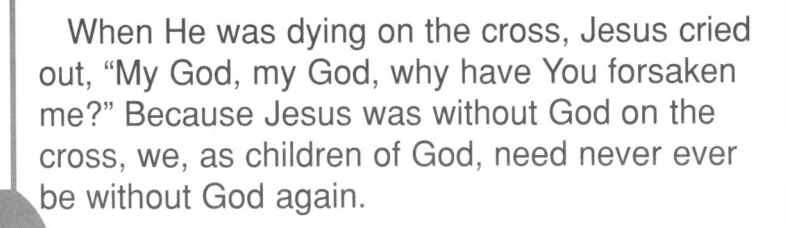

When He was dying on the cross, Jesus cried out, "My God, my God, why have You forsaken me?" Because Jesus was without God on the cross, we, as children of God, need never ever be without God again.

> Lord, thank You that You are always with me and that I need never feel alone.

You need never feel that you are alone, because God is always with you.

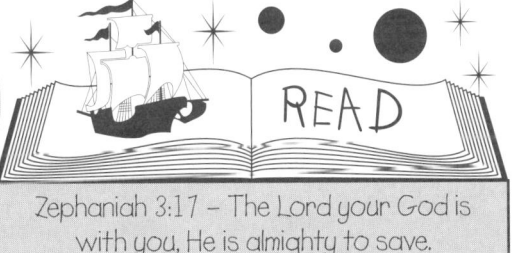

READ

Zephaniah 3:17 – The Lord your God is with you, He is almighty to save.

One of Jesus' names is Emmanuel. In Isaiah 9:5 we read about four other names Jesus has. What are they?

ANSWER: Wonderful Counsellor, Mighty God, Everlasting Father and Prince of Peace

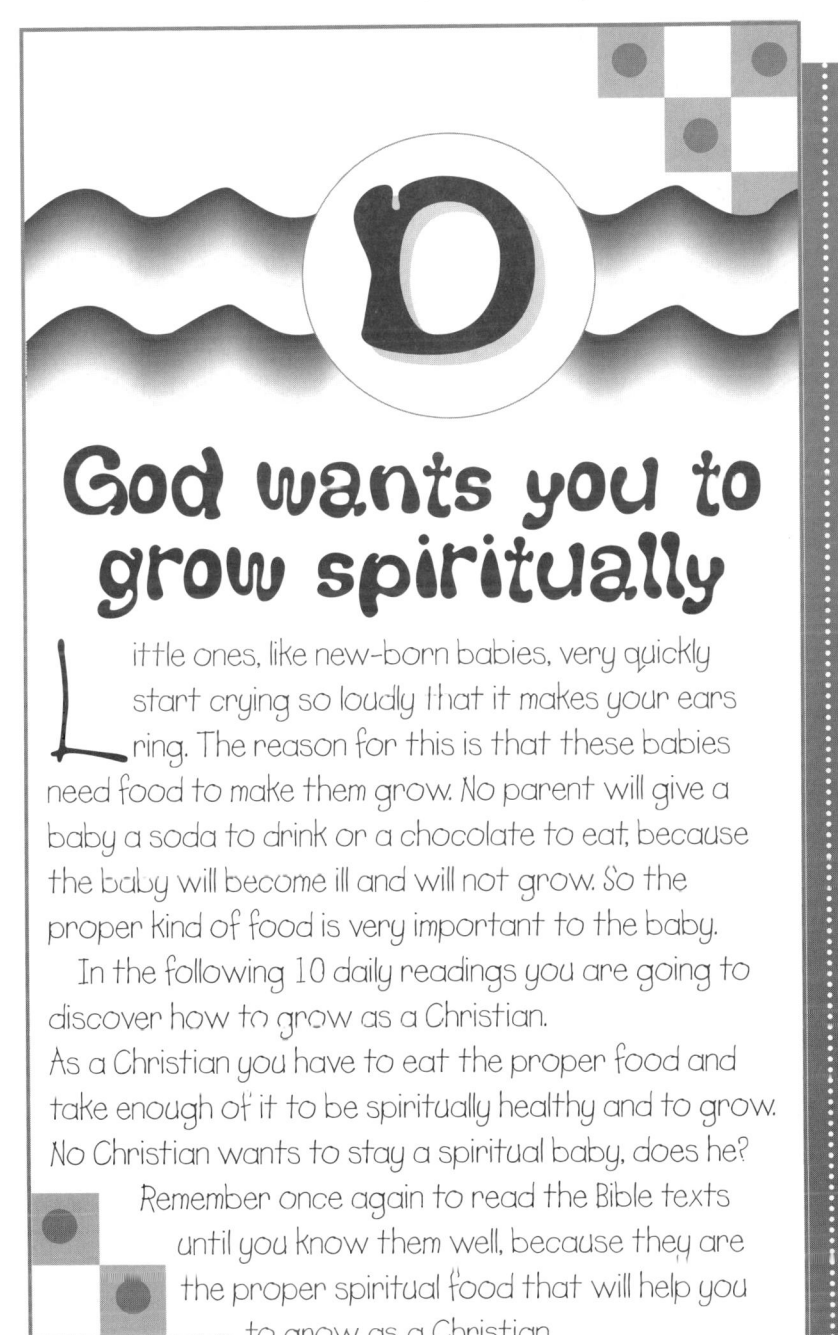

God wants you to grow spiritually

Little ones, like new-born babies, very quickly start crying so loudly that it makes your ears ring. The reason for this is that these babies need food to make them grow. No parent will give a baby a soda to drink or a chocolate to eat, because the baby will become ill and will not grow. So the proper kind of food is very important to the baby.

In the following 10 daily readings you are going to discover how to grow as a Christian.
As a Christian you have to eat the proper food and take enough of it to be spiritually healthy and to grow. No Christian wants to stay a spiritual baby, does he?

Remember once again to read the Bible texts until you know them well, because they are the proper spiritual food that will help you to grow as a Christian.

You can talk to God

One day two children – a brother and his sister – were playing with the two-way radios they were given for Christmas. Next moment Frank said something, but Cathy couldn't hear a thing. Then Cathy said something, but Frank couldn't hear her either. Soon they were shouting at each other. Then they realised something must be wrong with the radio's leads. When they went to see what was wrong, they found that the naughty dog had chewed off one of the leads.

Frank and Cathy were having a pleasant conversation over their two-way radios without being able to see each other. Although we can't see God, we can talk to Him any time of the day or the night. We don't even need a two-way radio. Neither is it necessary to make an appointment with Him. In James 4:8 He says that you may come near to Him at any time. He loves you so much that He wants you to talk to Him. He is always available. The communication line between you and God is always open. It never becomes busy or goes dead.

Lord, thank You that I can talk to You at any time – when things are good or bad at school, at home or on the sports field. Thank You for always listening to my prayers and answering them.

You can talk to God at any time.

READ

James 5:16 – The prayer of a righteous man is powerful and effective.

To which garden did Jesus go to pray just before He was crucified?

(Hint: Matthew 26:36)

ANSWER: Gethsemane

God gives you his whole creation

It was Christmas and Derek couldn't wait for the presents his father and mother were going to give him. Later only one present was lying under the Christmas tree and Derek knew it was the one he had bought for his mother. Had his father and mother forgotten about him? he wondered. Suddenly his father got up and walked to the kitchen with a broad smile. He returned with a big basket in his arms. "Here you are, Derek, with love from Mum and Dad." Derek took the basket eagerly and when he looked into it, he couldn't believe his eyes. He saw the most beautiful puppy lying in the basket. He was so excited. "Thank you, Dad, thank you, Mum!" he cried. "It's the most wonderful present I have ever received!" His father laughed and said, "I'm glad, Derek, but now you must look after it very well."

The Lord gives you an even bigger present than the one Derek had received – his whole creation. Genesis 1:26 says that God made man as his representative to rule over the fish, the animals and the plants. God wants you to take good care of his creation. That is why you must take good care of your pets. You must not throw rubbish around. Rather hand in plastic, paper and glass to be recycled.

Lord, thank You that I may rule over Your creation. Please help me to take good care of it.

As the ruler over God's creation you must take good care of his creation.

READ

Genesis 1:27   So God created man in his own image.

? Who was Adam's eldest son?

(Hint: Genesis 4:1)

ANSWER: Cain

God gives you his Word

One Friday afternoon the BMW belonging to Terence's father broke down on the road. On Saturday morning his father spent hours trying to repair the BMW. He became very frustrated, because he couldn't get it to run again. He read the manual and did exactly what they told him, but to no avail. The car wouldn't go. Terence picked up the manual and then started laughing. "Dad, you will never get the BMW going again, because this is the manual of mum's Toyota."

The Lord also gave you a manual to read to show you how you can live happily. In God's manual you can also read how good God is to you, in good and in bad times. Psalm 119:105 says that God's Word is like a lamp to your feet and a light for your path. Do not let things like the TV, videos and wrong friends tell you how to live. No, God has given you his Word so that you will know how to live properly. If you want to be really happy, read your Bible regularly and do what God tells you in his Word.

Lord, thank You for a valuable manual like the Bible. Thank You for everything I can learn from it. Please help me always to be faithful to your Word.

God's Word is your manual for a happy life.

READ

Psalm 119:133 – Direct my footsteps according to your word.

? Who was faithful to God even though it nearly cost him his son's life?
(Hint: Genesis 22:9)

ANSWER: Abraham

You want to tell

It was the beginning of a new term. Miss Borman found it hard to start with the schoolwork that day. The children in grade 6 couldn't stop talking about what they had done during the holidays.

After a few minutes Miss Borman got a chance to speak. "Class, we enjoy talking about all that had happened during the holidays. To me it seems as if we don't always talk as easily about what God has done in our lives. Barry, don't you want to tell us what happened to you on the SU camp?"

Barry got up shyly. "I am a bit shy, but I would like to tell you anyway. As you all know, I am quite a good boy. So I thought that I would one day go to heaven automatically. At the camp, however, I heard that we were all sinners. Suddenly I remembered that I sometimes lie and that I was envious of our rich neighbour. I was very sorry about all this and decided to give my whole life to God. We were also taught at camp that we must tell others about all the things that the Lord does for us."

What can you tell other people? That God loves both you and them. That Jesus died for both you and them on the cross. And that Jesus can forgive our sins.

Lord, I am also a little shy to talk about You. Give me the courage and the correct words.

God wants you to tell others about Him.

READ

Mark 16:15 – Go into all the world and preach the good news to all creation.

Who were the two people who, even when they were in jail, couldn't stop talking about the Lord?

(Hint: Acts 16 : 25)

ANSWER: Paul and Silas

God gives you spiritual food to grow

Peter and his friends were walking home after school. "Today we learnt that we have to eat food from all the food groups to stay healthy," said Anthony.

"Yuck!" said Peter. "I hate vegetables and fruit – sweets and chips can also give you energy. I wish I could have a packet of chips, sweet chocolate and a Coke for lunch."

"You're silly," said Anthony, "your body will never keep it up if you only eat junk food. Your teeth will rot, you will not be able to play rugby and your face will be full of pimples."

Just as your body needs healthy food, so does your spirit need healthy food to grow. You will never grow strong spiritually if you do not take in the proper spiritual food. What kind of food makes you grow spiritually? To pray and to read your Bible regularly makes you strong. When you visit places where you learn more about God, like the church, youth actions and SU meetings, you will become strong spiritually. And if you have friends who also love Jesus, they will build you up spiritually too.

In John 6:35 we read that Jesus is the bread that gives life. If we have Jesus in our lives, we will be healthy Christians.

Lord, please help me to take in the proper food to make me healthy and strong in spirit.

To grow strong in spirit, you need Jesus, the bread of life, in your life.

READ

John 6:35 – Then Jesus declared, "I am the bread of life. He who comes to me will never go hungry, and he who believes in me will never be thirsty."

How many times do we read about bread in John 6:26-40?

ANSWER: Seven times

The Bible is your light

One evening, just as the Jones family had finished their supper, the lights went off. Suddenly it was pitch-dark. "Elsa, please fetch a couple of candles from the kitchen," her mother said. Feeling her way, Elsa went to the kitchen. When she found the candles, she lit one immediately. "What wonderful things candles are," she said.

Later when they were reading in the Bible, her father said, "Just like these candles give us light, God has given us the Bible as a lamp. Just like the candles that showed you where to walk, Elsa, the Bible shows us what is right and what is wrong."

If you are not sure whether something is right or wrong, the Bible can help you with an answer. You are perhaps wondering whether it is wrong to desire your friend's new bicycle. Then you can read in Exodus 20:17 that it is wrong to desire something that belongs to someone else. Sometimes you wonder how a Christian should live. The answer to this you will also find in the Bible. Read Ephesians 4:25-32.

Lord, thank You that your Word tells me what is right and what is wrong. Please help me to listen to your Word.

In the Bible you can read about what is right and what is wrong.

Psalm 119:105 – Your Word is a lamp to my feet and a light for my path.

How many books are there in the Bible?

ANSWER: Sixty six

Jesus wants to use you

Pete said, "You know, Mother, during the children's service today the minister asked those of us who wanted to do something for Jesus, to stand up."

"And did you stand up, too?" his mother asked.

"But Mother, I am only in grade 5. How can the Lord Jesus use me? I am far too young."

"Pete, do you remember the story about the servant girl belonging to Naaman's wife? She was still very young. The Bible says that she was a little girl. But she was not ashamed of telling people that her God could do anything. If she had kept quiet, Naaman would never have recovered and never have learnt to know the Lord."

You are never too young to do something for the Lord. God has an important task for everyone who loves Him, whether they are young or old. We must tell people about God. Tell your friends when you have read a beautiful piece in the Bible or heard a good sermon. Share it with your friends when one of your prayers was answered. In this way you can be a witness for God, even though you are young.

Lord, I now know that You can use me, even though I am young. Show me how and where You want to use me.

Jesus has an important job for you, even though you are young.

READ

1 Timothy 4:12 – Don't let anyone look down on you because you are young, but set an example for the believers in speech, in life, in love, in faith and in purity.

? What kind of illness did Naaman have?

(Hint: 2 Kings 5:1)

ANSWER: He had leprosy

You can make time for God

Janine was a very busy girl. To be able to fit everything into her busy schedule, she drew up a timetable. Her timetable for Monday looked like this: 05:30 – jogging; 06:00 – bathing and dressing; 06:30 – breakfast and brushing teeth; 07:00 – going to school; 07:30 - 13:30 – school; 14:00 - 16:00 – lunch and homework; 16:30 - 17:30 – tennis lesson; 18:00 -19:00 – TV and supper; 19:00 - 20:00 – practising music; 20:00 - 21:00 – finish reading story book; 21:00 – go to bed. When she had finished drawing up her timetable, she realised that she hadn't fitted in any time for being quiet with God.

Sometimes our days are so filled with work and pleasure that we forget about God completely. He wants us to do these things, but He also wants us to spend time with Him.

When people are friends and have a relationship with each other, they make time for each other and talk to each other on a regular basis. When you have a relationship with God, it is also necessary to talk to Him and to read his Word regularly, in order to know exactly how precious you are to Him and what his will is for your life.

Lord, I am sorry that I don't always make room in my busy schedule for You. Please help me to devote enough time to You each day.

God wants you to spend time with Him.

READ

James 4:8 – Come near to God and He will come near to you.

How often did Daniel pray each day?

(Hint: Daniel 6 : 11)

ANSWER: Three times

Other people are also precious to God

Frank saw his friend Ben going outside with a full garbage bag. "What is in the bag, Ben?" Frank asked. "I have taken some rubbish from my room and want to throw it away. I am getting rid of all my tapes, because I only listen to CD's now. My father gave me a new tennis racket and now I am throwing the old one away."

"May I please have the tapes? I only have a cassette player and you have the most wonderful music. And you know, my little brother is dying for a racket – can we buy your old one?" Frank asked enthusiastically.

Stuff that seems like rubbish to some people, may be very important to others. Sometimes we treat people as though they were rubbish. Just because they are different from us, we ignore them and sometimes treat them badly. Remember that God does not make rubbish. He made each one of us for a very specific purpose, so all his creatures are important to Him.

Do you treat other people as if they are important? Whenever you come into contact with children who are not popular with you and your friends, remember that they are very precious to God and that He loves them as much as He loves you.

Lord, help me to remember that other people are also precious to You and that I have to treat everyone I come into contact with, with respect.

Each one of us is important to God, because He has a plan for each of us.

READ

1 Timothy 4:4 – For everything God created is good.

Fill in the missing words:

I now realise how true it is that God

_____

Acts 10:34

You can help with the harvest

Johnny and his father were sitting on a big combine. They had been harvesting for the past five days. "The corn is looking good this year, Son. We are going to have a very good crop," his father said.

"But what a big job it is to harvest, Dad," Johnny said, feeling very tired. "We work from early in the morning till late at night. Suppose we didn't have so many helpers? Then we would have lost a big part of the crop."

"That makes me think about the other harvest we read about in the Bible," his father said. "In Matthew 9:37 we read that the harvest is plentiful and the workers are few. This means that there are many people who still don't follow the Lord and that very few Christians are willing to go and tell them about the Lord."

The Lord loves all those people who still don't follow Him too. He doesn't want any one of them to be lost. Just as the workers gather corn, we who love God, have to lead people to Him. Because you are very precious to God, He can use you to be his witness. Are you willing?

Lord, I really want to help You with the big harvest. Make me strong to do it.

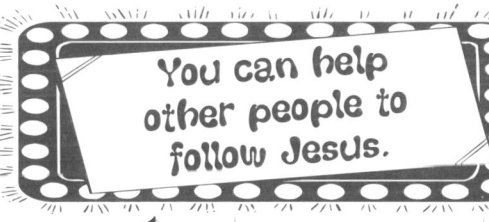

You can help other people to follow Jesus.

READ

Isaiah 6:8 – Then I heard the voice of the Lord saying, "Whom shall I send? And who will go for us?"

Paul helped to gather the harvest. Once he was stranded on the island Malta and there he started telling the people about the Lord. What narrow escape did he have on this island?
(Hint: Acts 28:1-6)

ANSWER:

His hand was bitten by a snake while he was putting wood on a fire, but he suffered no ill effects

E

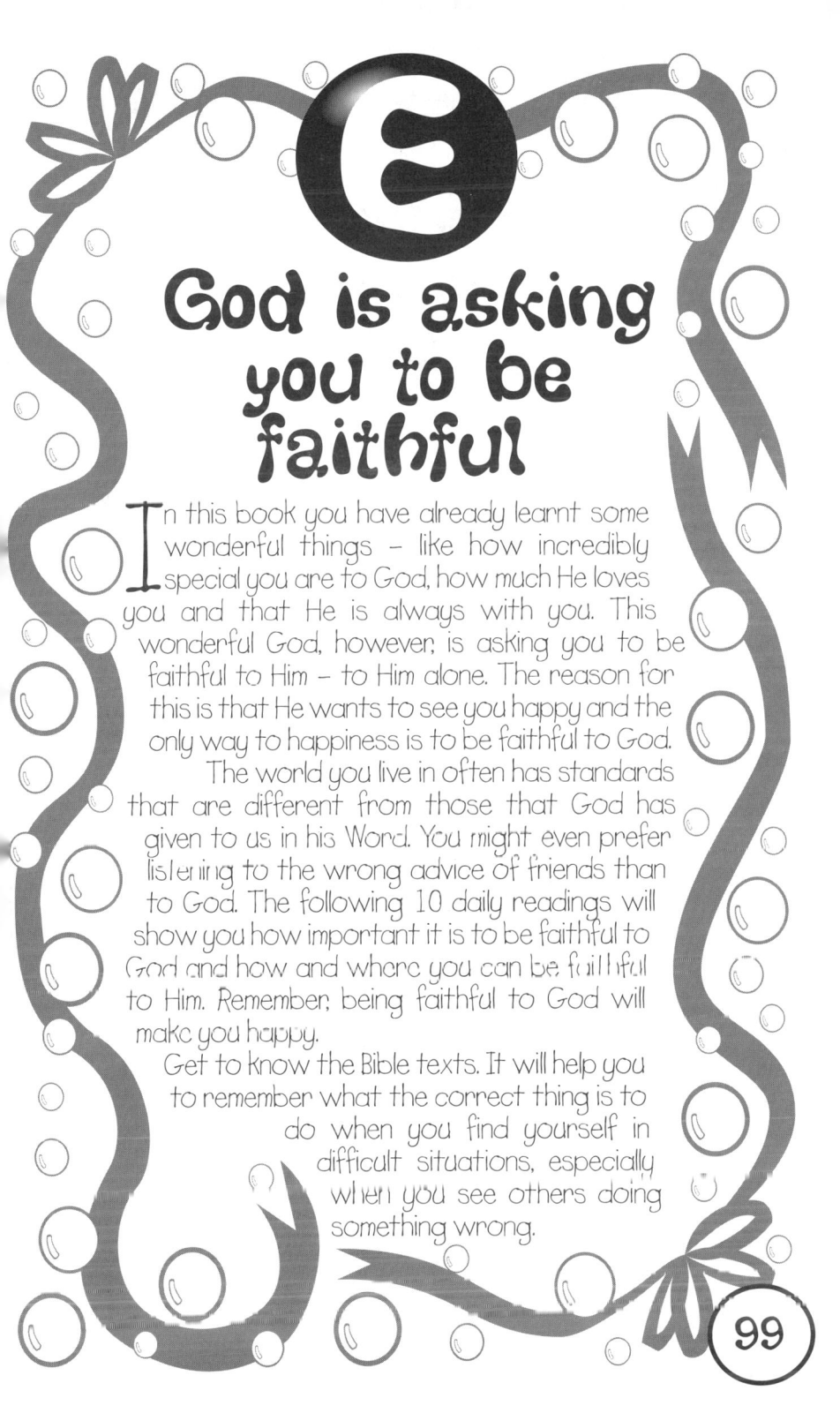

God is asking you to be faithful

In this book you have already learnt some wonderful things – like how incredibly special you are to God, how much He loves you and that He is always with you. This wonderful God, however, is asking you to be faithful to Him – to Him alone. The reason for this is that He wants to see you happy and the only way to happiness is to be faithful to God.

The world you live in often has standards that are different from those that God has given to us in his Word. You might even prefer listening to the wrong advice of friends than to God. The following 10 daily readings will show you how important it is to be faithful to God and how and where you can be faithful to Him. Remember, being faithful to God will make you happy.

Get to know the Bible texts. It will help you to remember what the correct thing is to do when you find yourself in difficult situations, especially when you see others doing something wrong.

You can make your own choices

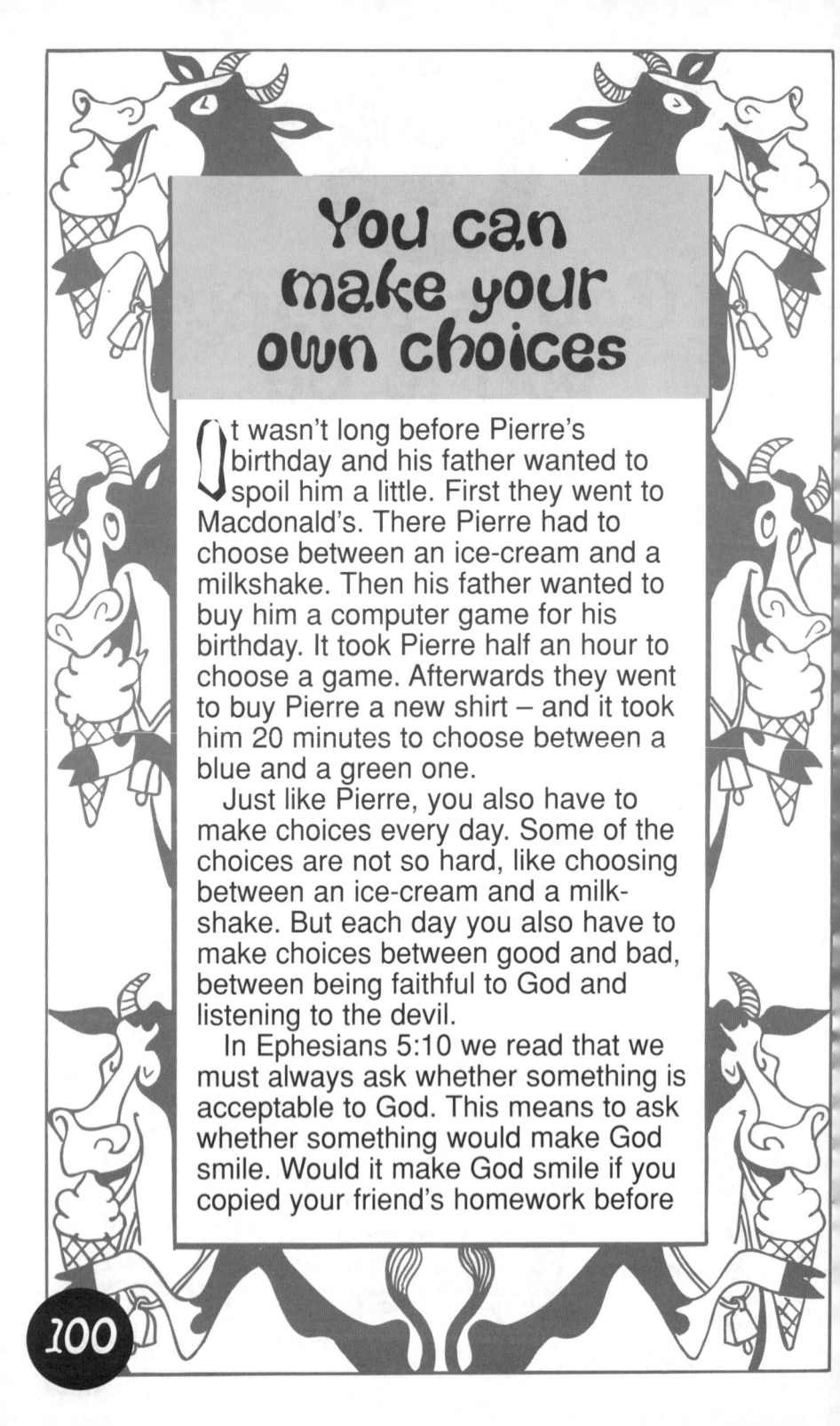

It wasn't long before Pierre's birthday and his father wanted to spoil him a little. First they went to Macdonald's. There Pierre had to choose between an ice-cream and a milkshake. Then his father wanted to buy him a computer game for his birthday. It took Pierre half an hour to choose a game. Afterwards they went to buy Pierre a new shirt – and it took him 20 minutes to choose between a blue and a green one.

Just like Pierre, you also have to make choices every day. Some of the choices are not so hard, like choosing between an ice-cream and a milkshake. But each day you also have to make choices between good and bad, between being faithful to God and listening to the devil.

In Ephesians 5:10 we read that we must always ask whether something is acceptable to God. This means to ask whether something would make God smile. Would it make God smile if you copied your friend's homework before school in the morning? Would it make God smile if you lied to your coach about why you had not been to the hockey or gymnastics practice? Your friends don't want to play with the new kid in class, because he looks like a nerd. But to you he appears lonely and you go and talk to him. Would this make God smile?

It's not always easy to make the correct choice, but because you are precious to God, He will help you to do it.

> Whenever you must make a choice, first ask yourself whether the choice you make will make God smile.

> Lord, please help me and guide me each day to make the correct choices. Help me always to choose that which will make You smile.

READ

Ephesians 5:10 – Find out what pleases the Lord.

Who was the man who killed an Egyptian? (Hint: Exodus 2:12)

ANSWER: Moses

God doesn't want you to use foul language

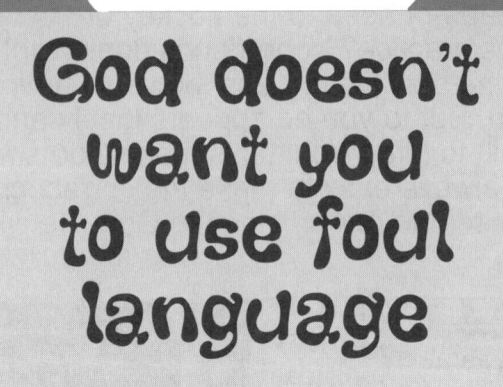

Switch on the TV and you'll often hear the people in the films and stories swearing. Some TV sets even have buttons you can push if you don't want to listen to all the swearing. Listen carefully at school how many of your schoolmates are swearing. Sometimes it is so bad that you want to put your hands over your ears. Yes, people go as far as using the Lord's name as a swear word.

Paul warns in Ephesians 4:29 that we must never let foul language come from our lips. That means that we may not even swear when we get a fright or when we are angry. No foul word may ever come from your mouth.

Paul tells us to choose our words in such a way that we will say only good things – words that build us up and not break us down. Foul language breaks us and other people down. That is why we must stay away from it as far as possible.

No foul language may come from your mouth.

Lord, please help me to never allow a foul word to cross my lips. Also help me to use the correct words when I talk to my friends about their swearing.

READ

Ephesians 4:29 – Do not let any unwholesome talk come out of your mouths, but only what is helpful for building others up according to their needs, that it may benefit those who listen.

Who cursed David?

(Hint: 1 Samuel 17)

ANSWER: Goliath

God wants you to live like Jesus

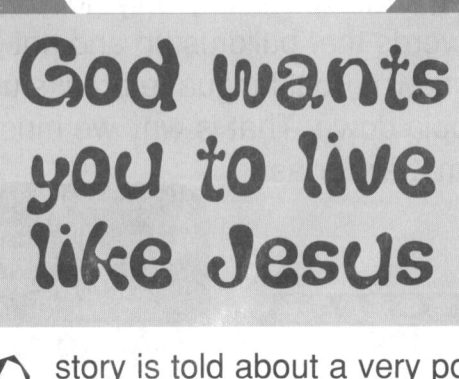

A story is told about a very poor little boy who lived in London. Some days his family had nothing to eat. Close to their flat there was a bakery that baked the most delicious bread and cakes. With longing eyes the little boy stood in front of the bakery each day and breathed in the lovely odour of freshly baked bread. One day a man saw the little boy standing outside. When he came out of the bakery, he gave the little boy a lovely fresh doughnut filled with cream. The little boy was very glad and then he timidly asked the man, "Are you perhaps Jesus?"

People long for someone like Jesus. We can try to fill his shoes here on earth. That is the reason why we should become more and more like Jesus. It sounds almost impossible, doesn't it? Jesus always acted lovingly and friendly when He was on earth. How can we succeed in becoming more like Him?

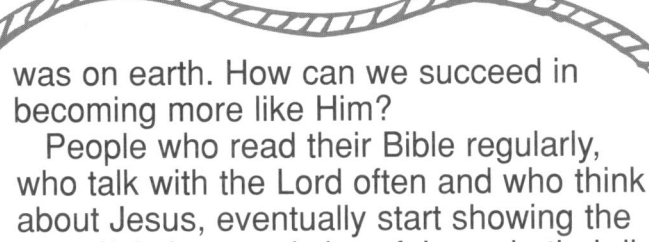

People who read their Bible regularly, who talk with the Lord often and who think about Jesus, eventually start showing the beautiful characteristics of Jesus in their lives. Some people wear bracelets to remind them they must act the way Jesus would have done. Who can help you become more and more like Jesus? The Holy Ghost that lives in you.

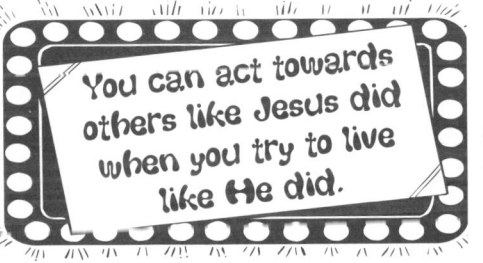

> You can act towards others like Jesus did when you try to live like He did.

> Holy Ghost, please help me to live like Jesus more and more every day.

READ

1 John 2:6 – Whoever claims to live in Him must walk as Jesus did.

? What must we do for each other if we want to be faithful to Jesus?

(Hint: John 13:14-15)

ANSWER: Wash each other's feet. This means to help and serve one another.

105

God is waiting for you at the finishing line

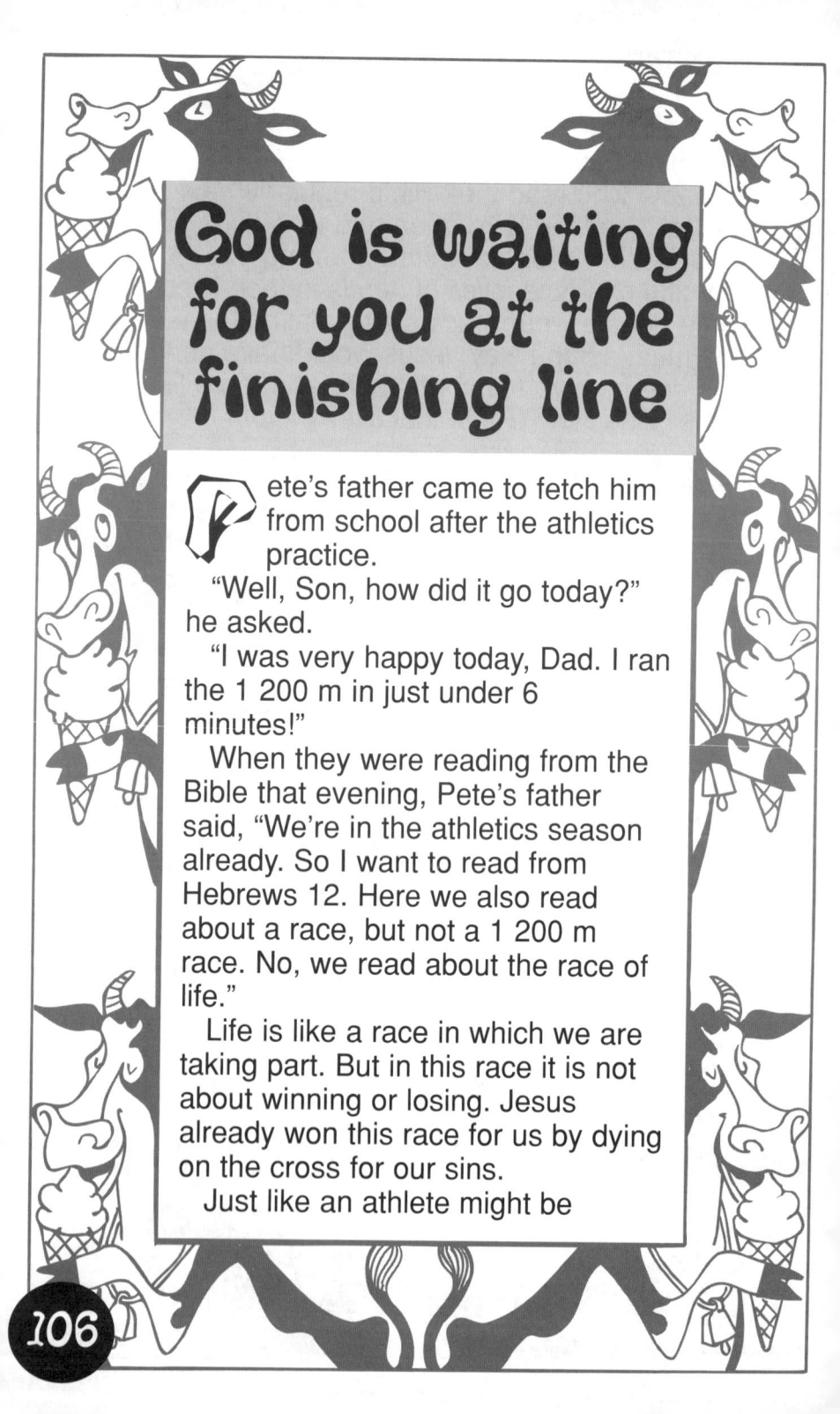

Pete's father came to fetch him from school after the athletics practice.

"Well, Son, how did it go today?" he asked.

"I was very happy today, Dad. I ran the 1 200 m in just under 6 minutes!"

When they were reading from the Bible that evening, Pete's father said, "We're in the athletics season already. So I want to read from Hebrews 12. Here we also read about a race, but not a 1 200 m race. No, we read about the race of life."

Life is like a race in which we are taking part. But in this race it is not about winning or losing. Jesus already won this race for us by dying on the cross for our sins.

Just like an athlete might be

hampered by an injury, for example, there are things that can hamper us in our race on earth – sin.

We can run our part of the race on earth by living like Jesus wants us to. In Hebrews 12:2 we read that we must keep our eyes on Jesus. Then we will win the prize. And the prize is to be with Jesus in heaven some day.

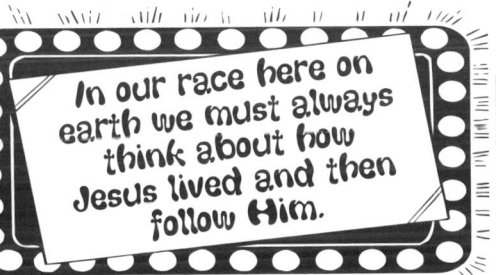

In our race here on earth we must always think about how Jesus lived and then follow Him.

Lord, help me to keep my eyes on You in this race here on earth.

READ

Hebrews 12:3 – Consider him who endured such opposition from sinful men, so that you will not grow weary and lose heart.

Read Philippians 3:14
What, according to you, is the "heavenly goal" Paul is talking about here?

ANSWER:
To be with Jesus in heaven one day

God wants you to speak the truth all the time

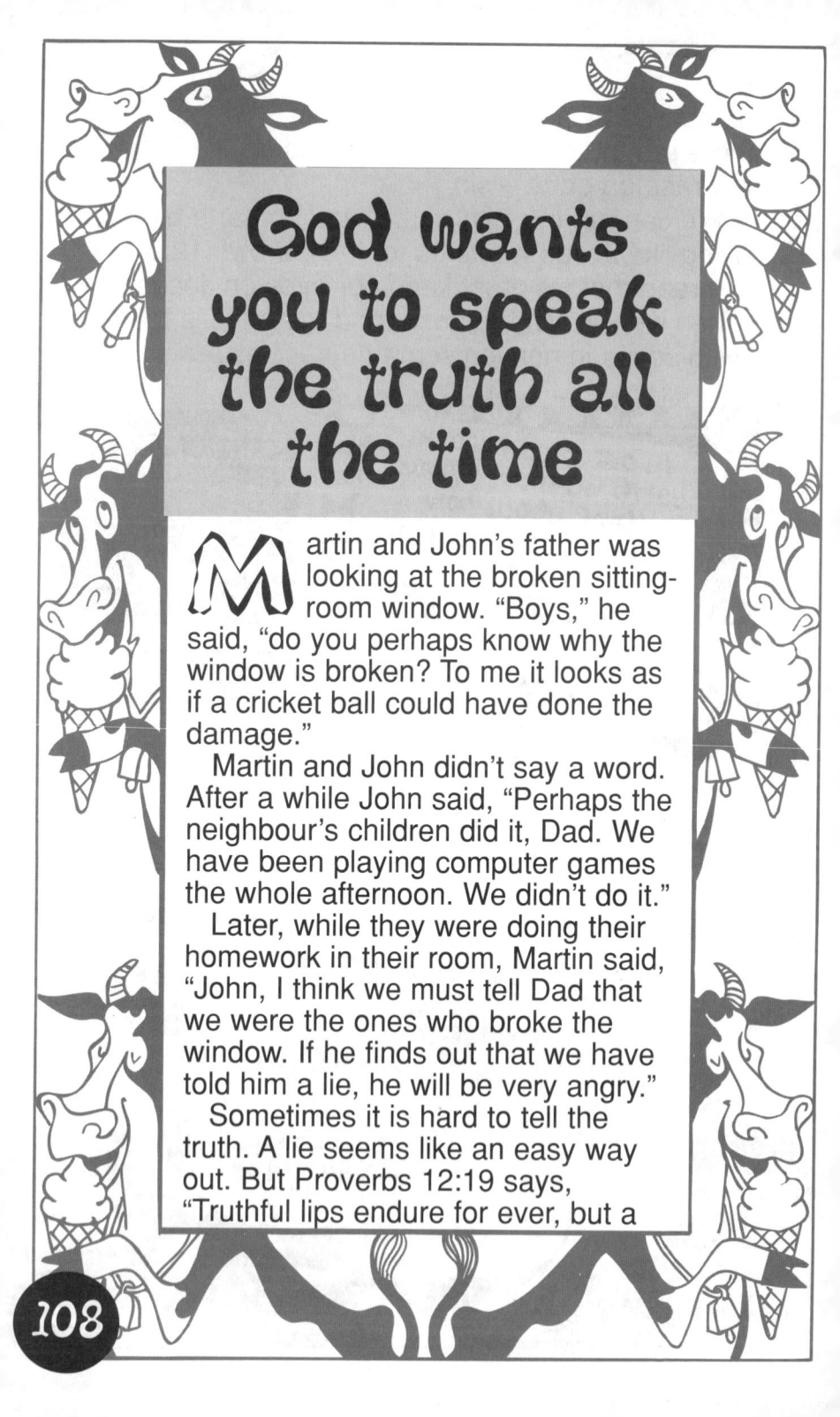

Martin and John's father was looking at the broken sitting-room window. "Boys," he said, "do you perhaps know why the window is broken? To me it looks as if a cricket ball could have done the damage."

Martin and John didn't say a word. After a while John said, "Perhaps the neighbour's children did it, Dad. We have been playing computer games the whole afternoon. We didn't do it."

Later, while they were doing their homework in their room, Martin said, "John, I think we must tell Dad that we were the ones who broke the window. If he finds out that we have told him a lie, he will be very angry."

Sometimes it is hard to tell the truth. A lie seems like an easy way out. But Proverbs 12:19 says, "Truthful lips endure for ever, but a lying tongue lasts only a moment." You can't hide your lies – they have an awful way of catching up with you.

We know that the Lord hates sin and therefore lies too. After you have given your whole life to Jesus, you must try not to tell lies any more. Ephesians 4:25 says, "Therefore each of you must put off falsehood and speak truthfully to his neighbour, for we are all members of one body."

Try to speak the truth all the time.

Lord, I am sorry for telling a lie once in a while. Help me to be honest all the time, even though it is hard.

READ

Proverbs 4:24 – Put away adversity from your mouth; keep corrupt talk far from your lips.

In Genesis 4:9 we read about someone who lied to the Lord. Who was it?

ANSWER: Cain

You need not be a chameleon

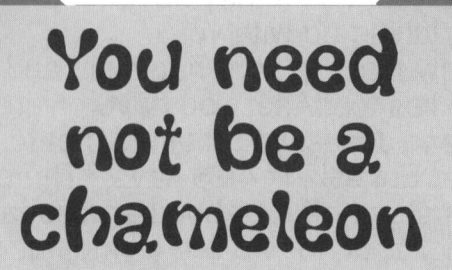

Chameleons are very interesting animals. When you look at one closely, you will see that it changes its colour to blend in with the surroundings. Experts say that chameleons do this to protect themselves. Their enemies can't catch them, because they can't see them.

It seems to me that we sometimes are like chameleons. We want to fit in with everything and everyone around us. It is important to us that our clothes look like those of our friends and that we act like they do. We will do anything not to be different. Perhaps we talk in a certain way at church, but completely differently when we are with friends who do not go to church.

It is much easier to be part of a group and to do what they are doing.

And it is very hard to stand alone. That is why we so easily give in to temptation in order to fit in with our surroundings, just like the chameleon.

We can, however, choose to say no when the group asks us to do things that are wrong. God wants us to live differently from the rest of the world.

> A child of God must be able to say no when the group wants to do something wrong.

> Lord, help me not to be like a chameleon, but to be strong when my friends want to do something that is wrong.

READ Romans 12:2 – Do not conform any longer to the pattern of the world.

Which of Jesus' disciples denied him?

(Hint: Mark 14:10)

ANSWER: Judas Iscariot

God wants you to live according to your beliefs

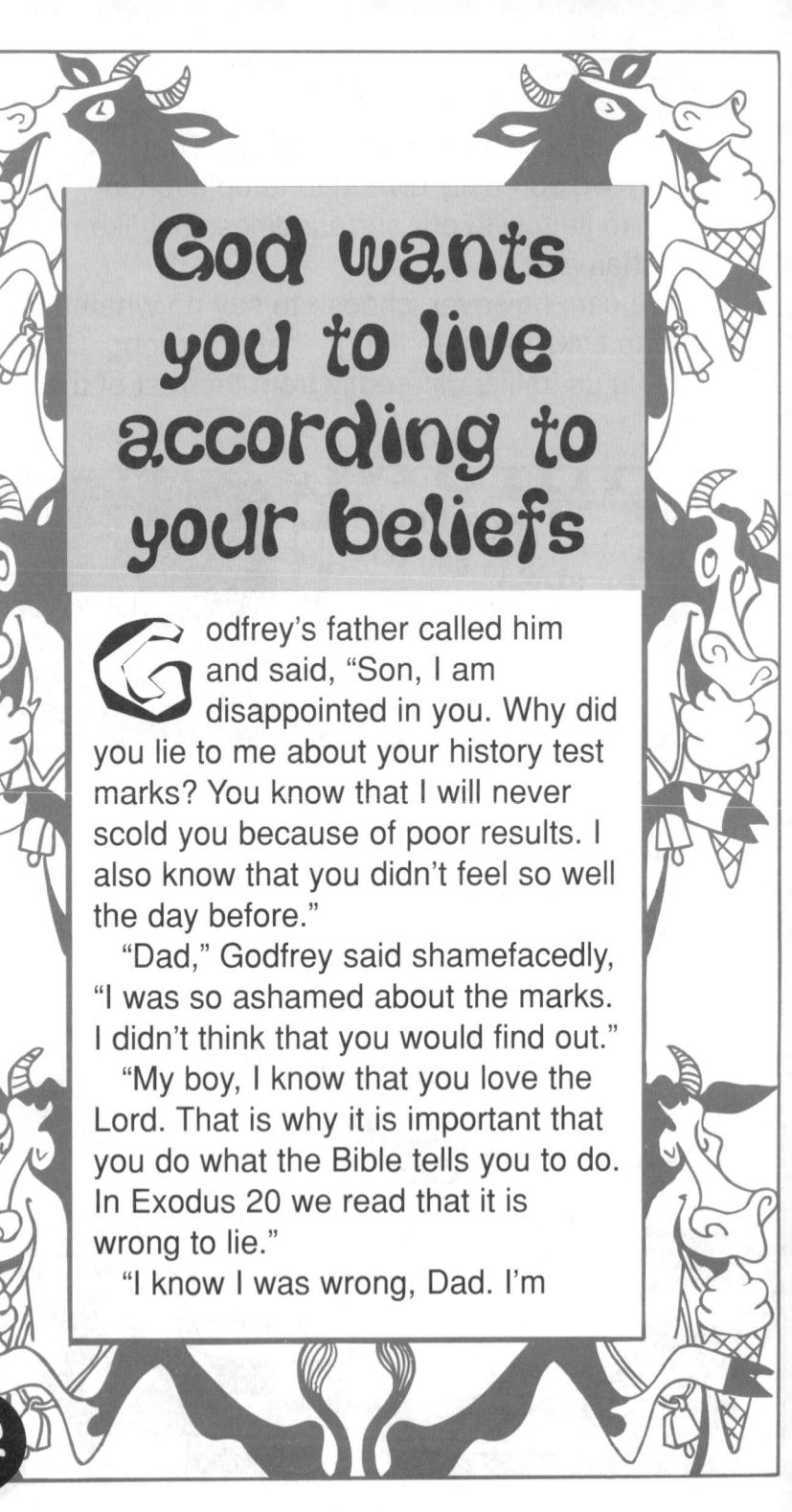

Godfrey's father called him and said, "Son, I am disappointed in you. Why did you lie to me about your history test marks? You know that I will never scold you because of poor results. I also know that you didn't feel so well the day before."

"Dad," Godfrey said shamefacedly, "I was so ashamed about the marks. I didn't think that you would find out."

"My boy, I know that you love the Lord. That is why it is important that you do what the Bible tells you to do. In Exodus 20 we read that it is wrong to lie."

"I know I was wrong, Dad. I'm

sorry. Actually I want my life to be a testimony to other people."

When you believe in Jesus, other people must be able to see it in your life. In James 2:17 we read that when faith is not accompanied by action, it is dead. It is a good thing to read the Bible and to believe what it says, but it is just as important to do what the Word tells us. If you don't live what you believe, your faith means nothing.

Live your faith.

Lord, help me not only to believe, but to believe and to act.

READ

Philippians 1:27 – Whatever happens, conduct yourselves in a manner worthy of the gospel of Christ.

With what does James 2:26 compare faith that does not go over in deeds?

ANSWER: With a body that is without spirit

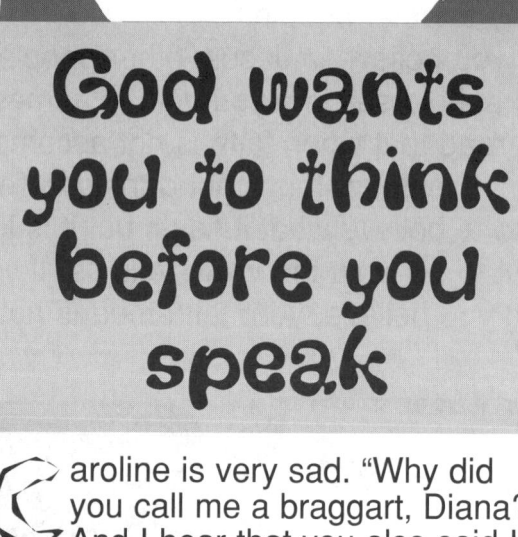

God wants you to think before you speak

Caroline is very sad. "Why did you call me a braggart, Diana? And I hear that you also said I think I'm cool because I do well in class. You are my best friend and it hurt me a lot," Caroline said.

"I'm very sorry, Caroline. I was jealous of you. I should have thought before I spoke."

Often one says something before you think – something that can hurt someone else very much. When you have said something bad, you can't take it back. In James 3:6 the tongue is compared with a fire. James says that a small spark can set a great forest on fire. In the same way something unimportant that you have said without thinking, can have negative consequences – you may lose your best friend.

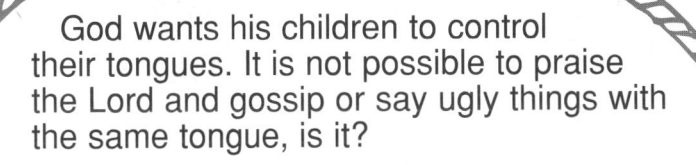

God wants his children to control their tongues. It is not possible to praise the Lord and gossip or say ugly things with the same tongue, is it?

We can hurt other people badly by what we say. God wants his children to control their tongues.

Lord, I am sorry for having hurt other people with what I said. Please help me to think before I speak.

READ

James 3:5 – Likewise the tongue is a small part of the body, but it makes great boasts.

Complete the following text:

Can a fig tree bear _____, or a grapevine bear _____? Neither can a salt spring produce _____.
(James 3:12)

You are a house in which God is living

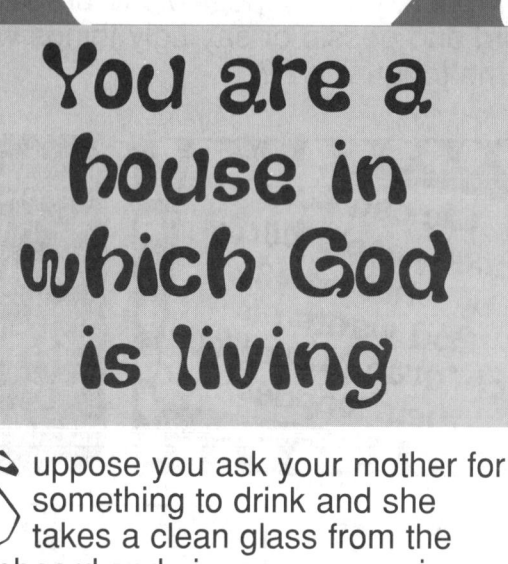

Suppose you ask your mother for something to drink and she takes a clean glass from the cupboard and gives you some ice-cold fruit juice. Would you drink it? Of course! Suppose the following happens: You ask your mother for something to drink and she gives you ice-cold fruit juice, but in a dirty glass that was standing on the sink. Would you drink it? No, I'm sure you would find it revolting.

Do you like using a dirty bathroom or sleeping in a dirty bed? No! Most people shudder when they just see something dirty.

Sometimes we forget that sin also makes us dirty. The Holy Ghost lives in the children of God, according to 1 Corinthians 3:16. Do you think He likes living in a dirty house?

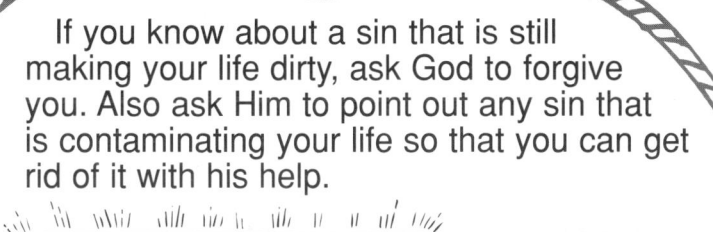

If you know about a sin that is still making your life dirty, ask God to forgive you. Also ask Him to point out any sin that is contaminating your life so that you can get rid of it with his help.

You are like a house in which God lives. Try to keep this house clean and holy.

Lord, I know that your Holy Spirit lives in me. I am sorry that sin sometimes makes my life so dirty. Please forgive me so that my life can be clean again.

READ

1 Corinthians 3:16 – Don't you know that you yourselves are God's temple and that God's Spirit lives in you?

Make a list of the sins which you think are making your life dirty. Ask God to forgive you for these sins. Then tear up the piece of paper and throw it away. Believe that, just like you tore up and threw away the piece of paper, God forgives you your sins and erases them.

God wants you to build your life on Him

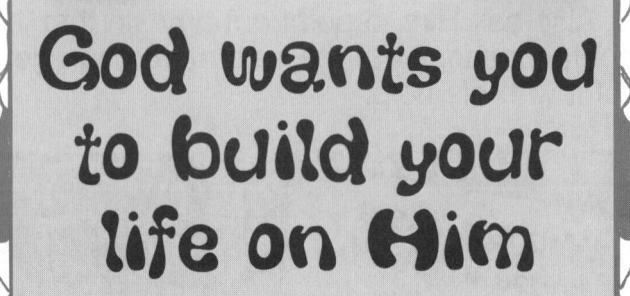

It is so good to hear well-known sports stars or other famous people openly confess their love for the Lord. Someone like Penny Heyns, the famous swimmer, and Elana Meyer, the athlete, are but two of the famous stars who are not ashamed of telling everyone that God is the rock on which they build their lives.

But there are many people who build their lives on the talents that God had given them. Some sing beautifully or are good athletes, but this can't last forever. What are they going to do when they are not able to use this talent any more?

That is why the Lord tells you in Matthew 7:24 that you must be like a wise man who builds his house on a rock. By being faithful to God and his

Word, you are building on God as your rock – and this will last forever. A fool is someone who doesn't build his house on the Lord, but on all kinds of other things that earn him honour and respect. Being unfaithful to God is like building a house on sand. It will not last. It is temporary and will someday just disappear.

Build your life on God by being faithful to Him.

Lord, please help me to build my life on You, my rock. Help me to know when I am building it on the wrong stuff.

READ

Proverbs 8:32 – Now then, my sons, listen to me; blessed are those who keep my ways.

Who is the man we read about in 1 Samuel 7:13 who built on the Lord as his rock?

ANSWER: Samuel

God is with you when you suffer

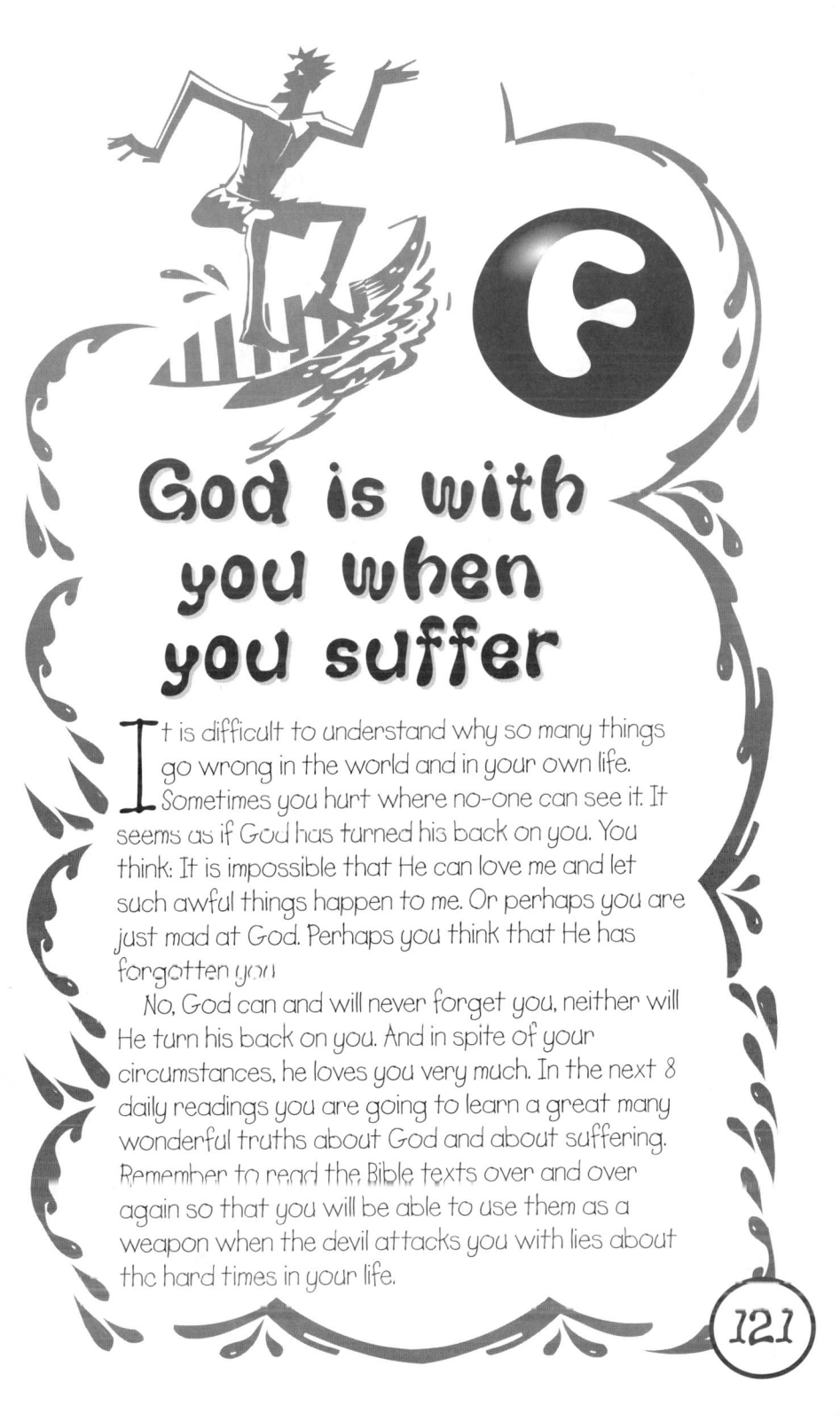

It is difficult to understand why so many things go wrong in the world and in your own life. Sometimes you hurt where no-one can see it. It seems as if God has turned his back on you. You think: It is impossible that He can love me and let such awful things happen to me. Or perhaps you are just mad at God. Perhaps you think that He has forgotten you.

No, God can and will never forget you, neither will He turn his back on you. And in spite of your circumstances, he loves you very much. In the next 8 daily readings you are going to learn a great many wonderful truths about God and about suffering. Remember to read the Bible texts over and over again so that you will be able to use them as a weapon when the devil attacks you with lies about the hard times in your life.

Hand your crisis over to God

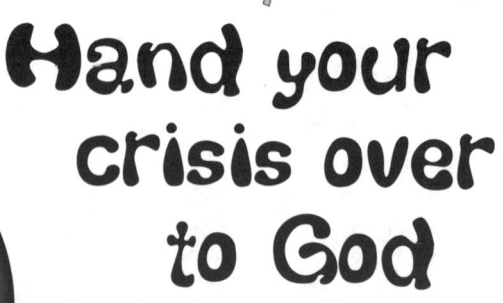

Susan and Louise were lying on their backs on the lawn. "Do you know, Susan," said Louise, "since my parents have become divorced, I feel sorry for children whose parents are in the middle of a divorce."

"It must have been hard for you," Susan answered. "How did you do it?"

"I talked to my grandmother about it. She helped me a lot. She also told me to talk to Jesus about the divorce and to tell Him how I feel about it."

Sometimes bad things happen to you. Your parents are getting a divorce. Someone whom you love very much dies. You are not elected for the rugby team. You don't do well in the exam. None of us can side-step crises. And in a crisis you can:
- run away;
- get mad at God;
- talk to someone you trust, or
- look for help from God and his Word.

It would not have been very clever to choose the first two options. The last two options, however, could help you a lot when you are going through a crisis.

> Lord, thank You very much that I can talk to You whenever I am in a crisis.

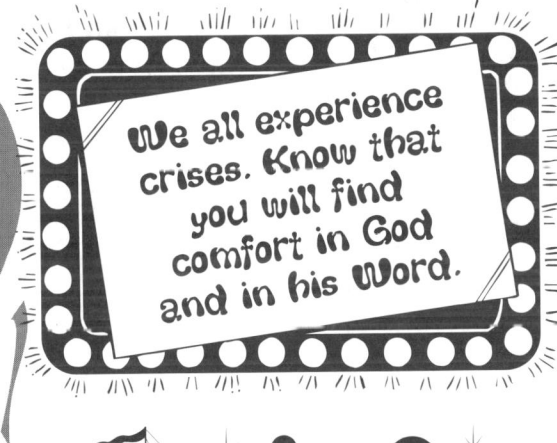

We all experience crises. Know that you will find comfort in God and in his Word.

READ

2 Corinthians 1:3(b) – (He is) the Father of compassion and the God of all comfort, who comforts us in all our troubles.

In the Bible we read about people who have also experienced crises. Someone has even been thrown off a ship and swallowed by a huge fish. Who was this?

ANSWER: Jonah

A crisis can make you strong

Can one make tea with lukewarm water? Of course not! To make a strong cup of tea, you need boiling water. Water that is so hot that you would burn your finger if you put it in the water. Yes, what the tea bag needs to brew strong tea, can burn your finger.

The bad things that sometimes happen to us make us feel as though we have landed in boiling water, like the tea bag. But, just as the tea bag becomes useful only when it is put in boiling water, Jesus can use the bad things that happen to us to make us strong. When bad things happen to us, we realise how badly we need Jesus in our lives. We see that we can only get through a crisis with his strength. And then other people can also see Jesus' strength in our lives. And after having gone through some crisis, we are able to help other people when they are experiencing that same crisis. This is what 2 Corinthians 1:4 tells us. If your grandmother or grandfather has died, you can help your friends when the same thing happens to them.

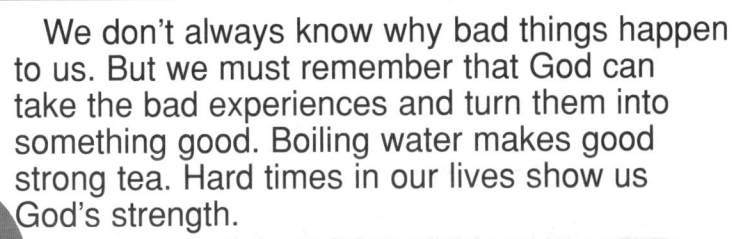

We don't always know why bad things happen to us. But we must remember that God can take the bad experiences and turn them into something good. Boiling water makes good strong tea. Hard times in our lives show us God's strength.

> Lord, I don't always know why bad things happen to me. Thank You that I can know You will be with me in these bad experiences.

When bad things happen to you, it can turn you into a stronger person.

READ

2 Corinthians 1:4 – ...who comforts us in all our troubles, so that we can comfort those in any trouble with the comfort we ourselves have received from God.

? In the Bible we read about a man who went through very hard times, but he never lost his faith in God. Read Job 42:5: "My ears had heard of You but now my eyes have seen you." Who was saying these words?

ANSWER: Job

You can be happy even though you are going through a bad time.

I know a very special woman, Aunt Gertrude. Her life has been very hard. One of her children died when he was still very young and she and her husband had to turn over every cent twice. They could only afford what was absolutely necessary. A short while ago she fell and broke her hip. I decided to go and visit her in the hospital. She was going through such a bad time and I was sure that she would need my encouragement. What a surprise I had when I reached the hospital and found Aunt Gertrude there laughing, yes, happy as usual. The nurses couldn't stop talking about this friendly, cheerful woman. When I asked her how she managed to stay cheerful in spite of her difficult circumstances, she answered, "My child, I know the Lord and no-one can take that away from me. He is taking care of me every day. How can I be depressed?"

Often we are down in the dumps when we are going through bad times. We blame other people, even God, for our unhappiness.

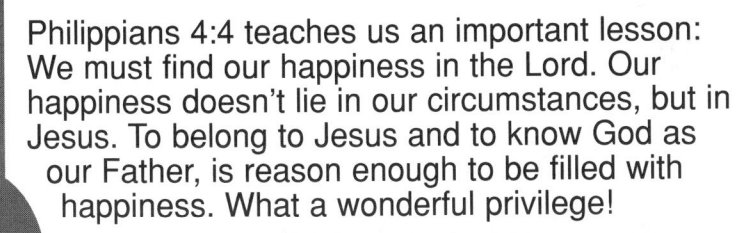

Philippians 4:4 teaches us an important lesson: We must find our happiness in the Lord. Our happiness doesn't lie in our circumstances, but in Jesus. To belong to Jesus and to know God as our Father, is reason enough to be filled with happiness. What a wonderful privilege!

> Lord, thank You that I do not have to look for my happiness in worldly possessions. Thank You that my happiness lies in the fact that I belong to Jesus.

You can be happy in the Lord, even when you are having a bad time.

READ

Philippians 4:4 – Rejoice in the Lord always. I will say it again: Rejoice!

? Who reached Jesus' open grave first and saw that it was empty?

(Hint: John 20:1)

ANSWER: Mary Magdalene

God carries you when you are going through a bad time

Little John-John loved rugby. He wished that he could play rugby every day. Game after game he gave his utmost when he had to dive, pass the ball to his team-mates or run flat out. One day he was going for the try-line, flat out as usual. His father was standing next to the field and was shouting, "Flat out, John-John, flat out!" The next moment John-John fell. He grabbed his ankle and one look at his face clearly showed that he was in great pain. He had sprained his ankle. His father ran onto the field, comforted him, picked him up and carried him off the field.

In the same way it sometimes happens that deep in our hearts we can get badly hurt. Someone gossips about you, a teacher scolds you severely or a friend speaks badly of you. This is not like a sprained ankle which shows where it hurts. You only know that your heart is very, very sore.

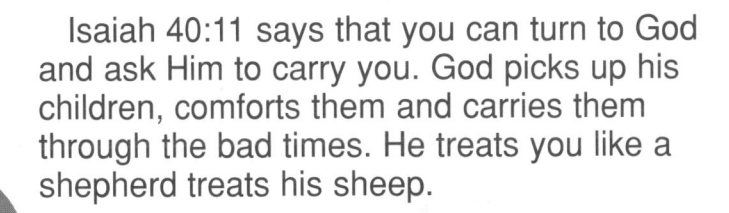

Isaiah 40:11 says that you can turn to God and ask Him to carry you. God picks up his children, comforts them and carries them through the bad times. He treats you like a shepherd treats his sheep.

Thank You, Lord, that I may come to You when I am going through a hard time. Thank You for comforting and carrying me.

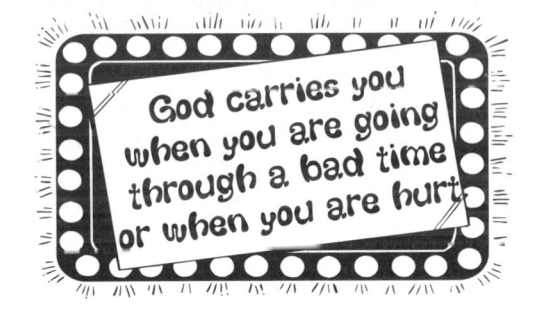

God carries you when you are going through a bad time or when you are hurt.

READ

Isaiah 63:9b - ... he lifted them up and carried them all the days of old.

Who was afraid when he heard that the enemy was on its way? What did he do then?
(Hint: 2 Chronicles 20 : 3 and 6)

ANSWER: Jehoshaphat. He prayed to God.

Suffering is not God's punishment for you

Frank and his little sister went shopping with their mother. It was Friday afternoon and there were lots of people. They were behaving very badly and their mum had to talk to them all the time and tell them to stay close to her. She was afraid that they would get lost in the crowd. The next moment Frank chased his sister around one of the shelves. When he had caught her and they returned to where their mother had been, she was gone. Both of them were very frightened and thought that this was their mother's way of punishing them. She had talked and talked, and now she was gone. They wouldn't listen, Frank thought sadly. But suddenly their mother came walking round the corner, crying. She took her children in her arms and hugged them. She had been so afraid that she would never find them again – while they were thinking that she was punishing them because she was mad at them.

We often go through hard times in our lives. Someone we love dies or becomes very ill. Perhaps you think it was because God doesn't love you and that he was punishing you. That is not true. God loves you all the time. Sometimes He wants to test your love for Him. He wants to make sure that you really love him, even though you are suffering. 1 Peter 1:6-7 tells us so. God doesn't want you to love Him only when things are going well. What He really wants, is that you must know that He loves you very much, especially in bad times.

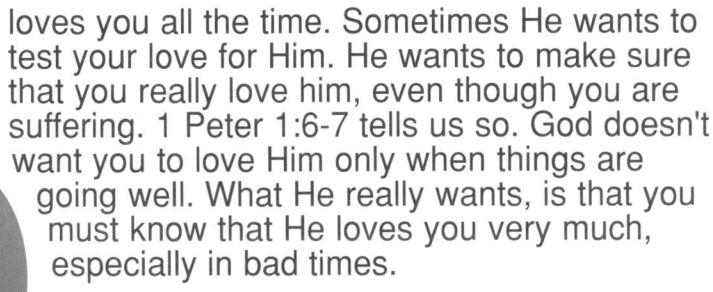

> Lord, thank You that You always love me. Thank You that I may know that the bad things that happen to me are not meant as a punishment for me.

God doesn't punish you by making you suffer. Perhaps He is only testing you to find out whether you really love Him.

READ

Lamentations 3:33 – For He does not willingly bring affliction or grief to the children of men.

Write down below how Jesus also had to suffer. (Hint: Read Mark 15:19-20)

Suffering can be your own fault

William was a good athlete. One evening he had to run the 1 200 m for his school during an important athletics meeting. His father had promised to buy him a big McDonald's burger after the race. He was trying to persuade William not to eat too much before the race. Unfortunately William didn't listen, and he and his friends stuffed themselves with candy-floss and chocolate. When the shot rang out, William was feeling rather heavy and after the first round he was getting nauseous. This turned out to be his worst race of the year – and it was his own fault.

Your suffering often is your own fault too. The consequences of doing something bad are never pleasant, but still we often make the wrong choices. Isaiah 59:2 tells us that our sins cause a separation between God and us. When we are separated from God, we can't be happy.

Fortunately you know that God

will forgive you. You can go to Him and tell Him that you're sorry. He will forgive you. Our God is not a God who stays angry and keeps on holding us responsible for our sins.

> Lord, forgive me for allowing sin to come into my life and so cause my own suffering. Thank You for forgiving me and that You love me unconditionally.

Suffering can be your own fault, but God loves you so much that He forgives you every time.

READ

Isaiah 59:2 – But your iniquities have separated you from your God.

Fill in the missing words:
Though your sins were like _____,
they shall be white as _____;
though they are red as crimson,
they shall be like _____.
(Isaiah 1:18)

God sees your tears

Anita hugged her friend, Betsy, who was crying. Then she said, "Betsy, I wanted to die when Miss Allen scolded you without reason this morning. I saw your tears and I was so sorry for you."

Just as the observant Anita had noticed her friend's tears, God also sees our suffering and our sorrows. Why did Anita notice Betsy's tears? Because she cared, of course. Because we are so precious to God, He notices our sorrows.

Are you also sad about something? Perhaps someone you love died. Perhaps your parents are divorced. Perhaps your best friend doesn't want to be friends with you any more. We live in a broken world with much sorrow. In Psalm 56:9 we read that God sees our tears and writes them down in his book.

Tell God about all the things that make you sad. Because He loves you, He wants to comfort you. He can do anything and He can help you. And remember, you have something wonderful to look forward to: Some day, in heaven, no-one will be sad any more. Isn't this fantastic news?

> Lord, thank You very much that You notice my sorrow and that I can talk to You about it.

Because you are precious to God, He notices when you are sad. You can also talk to Him about your sorrow.

READ

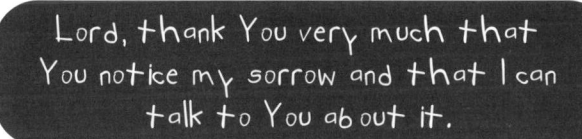

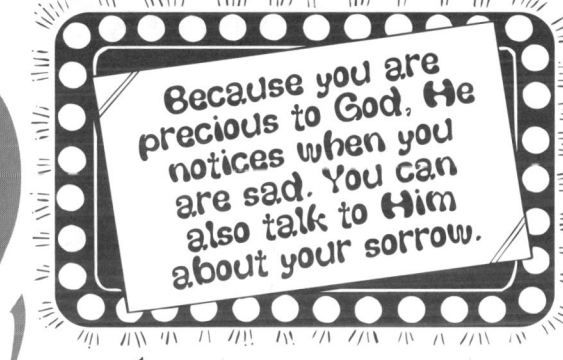

Revelation 21:4 – He will wipe every tear from your eyes. There will be no more death or mourning or crying or pain, for the old order of things has passed away.

In Mark 5 from verse 21 we read about someone's little daughter who died. Jesus told the people that they mustn't cry over her. She was not dead, she was only sleeping. Who was the father of this little girl?

ANSWER: Jairus

135

To be a Christian isn't always easy

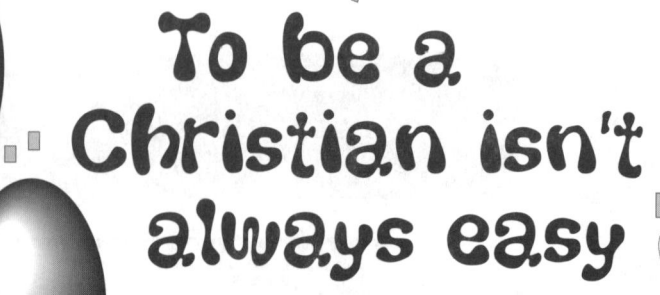

During the June holidays Billy attended a wonderful spiritual camp. When he arrived home afterwards, he received the bad news that their house had been broken into and that his favourite cricket bat had been stolen. Straight after the holidays he heard that his mathematics marks had dropped by 20%. Life really wasn't any fun! Many people think that being a child of God is easy. They think that bad things don't happen to Christians. Wrong! Children of God live in the world, but they are not of the world.

The Lord tells us in Psalm 23:4 that children of God can also experience bad times. But He also assures us that He will always be there to carry us through these times. He doesn't leave us on our own when we suffer. You can be sure that the Lord is near you, especially when you are suffering.

> Thank You, Lord, it is not always easy to be your child. Thank You that I can know that You will carry me through these dark periods.

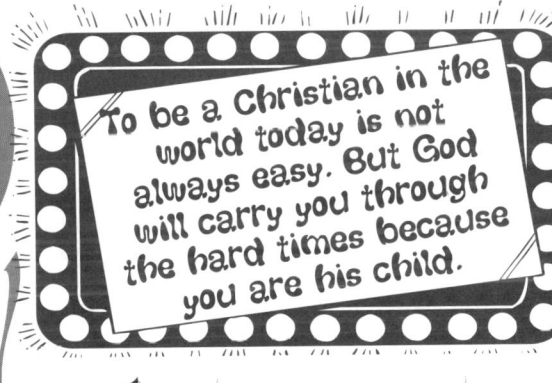

To be a Christian in the world today is not always easy. But God will carry you through the hard times because you are his child.

READ

Psalm 23:4 – Even though I walk through the valley of the shadow of death, I will fear no evil, for You are with me.

According to Psalm 27:1 the Lord is two things in times of darkness. What are these two things?

ANSWER: My light and my salvation

The cross is meant for you

The cross stands in the centre of Christian religion. Had there been no Jesus and no cross, there would have been no Christian religion today. Had there been no cross and no resurrection, there wouldn't have been anything like forgiveness, salvation and eternal life. God proves his great love for you through Jesus and the cross.

The cross opened the way for you to God. There was a time when we were separated from God because of our sins, but Jesus and the cross made it possible to be friends with God again. The following 10 daily readings will tell you about the fundamental truths of the cross. You are going to enjoy these daily readings. They contain many truths that can change your life for ever. Try to remember the Bible text given with each reading, because each of them contains some important truths about the cross.

The cross was meant for you

Have you ever thought what would happen if Robert, one of your classmates, did something wrong – like stealing an examination paper? Imagine the picture: The headmaster hears about it and rushes into the classroom. He is angry and asks in a loud voice who the culprit is. To everyone's surprise Gerard gets up slowly. Everybody knows he isn't guilty, but he is standing there in Robert's place. This means that the headmaster is going to punish Gerard instead of Robert. You have never heard of something like this, have you? It is the most wonderful thing you have ever experienced, that someone can do something like this for somebody else – to be punished in his place.

The Word of God explains very clearly in 2 Corinthians 5:21 that Jesus was without sin. You and I are the sinners. But because God loves us so much, He gave us a second chance. He let Jesus die on the cross for our sins. Isn't it the most wonderful thing that had ever happened and will ever happen? Jesus died on the cross in your place. He carried all your sins on the cross and was punished instead of you.

To show how grateful you are, God wants you to give your whole life to Jesus. Make Jesus the King of your life. By doing this, God makes you his child and you receive eternal life as a gift from Him.

Jesus, thank You for loving me so much that You died for me on the cross. I now give You my whole life. Please forgive me my sins. Thank You that I may be your child from now on.

Jesus died on the cross in your place.

READ

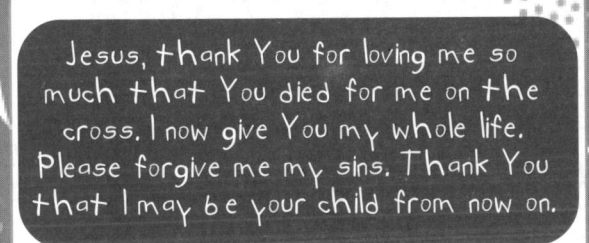

Colossians 1:14 -- ... the Son ... in whom we have redemption, the forgiveness of sins.

Write your name in the empty spaces below:

God made Him who had no sin to be sin for _____, so that in Him _____ might become the righteousness of God.

(2 Corinthians 5:21)

God loves you so much that...

Mrs Peterson was standing in a big shopping centre together with hundreds of other people. She had entered a competition where you could win a car and the winner was going to be announced at any minute. Hundreds of people had also entered their names. The box containing the entries was full. The announcer approached, holding the box with the entries. The shop manager put his hand deep into the container, shuffled the entries around and pulled out the lucky number. Mrs Peterson stood there wondering who the lucky person would be. She didn't even look at the number on her ticket. No-one stepped forward. The announcer repeated the number. For the first time Mrs Peterson looked at the card in her hand and then shouted in excitement – she had the winning number. She had won the car.

In John 3:16 we read that God so loved the world that He sent Jesus to die for the world's sins. When you read and hear this, you might think about all the people living far away in other countries. Perhaps you are thinking that what Jesus did, was meant for other people only. No, God's intention is that you and I must know that we are also from this "world". Jesus died on the cross – for you too. You are the world. That is why you can give your whole life to God out of gratitude for what Jesus did for you on the cross.

Lord, thank You that I may know that I am a part of the world. Thank You that Jesus also died for me. Forgive me my sins and make me your faithful child.

You are a part of this world for which Jesus died on the cross.

READ

John 3:16 – For God so loved the world that he gave his one and only Son, that whoever believes in him shall not perish but have eternal life.

Write your name in the empty spaces below:
God so loved _____ that He gave his only Son, that _____ who believes in Him, shall not perish, but have eternal life.
(John 3:16)

The cross is for forgiveness

Dogs have this bad habit of rolling in sand. Don't even mention how dirty they can be after it has rained. And to give a big, hairy dog a bath, is one of the funniest things you can do. In the process you get very wet and dirty too. But one good bath later – even though both you and the dog are wet – the dog looks brand new.

Just as a dog gets dirty from rolling in the sand, sin makes us dirty on the inside. The Bible teaches us in Psalm 51:7 that we were sinners even before we were born. So everyone is a sinner and has a sinful nature. To get to heaven, we need to be freed (delivered) from our sinful natures. "How do we do that?" you immediately ask. "What must I do to get rid of my sinful nature?"

The wonderful news is that Jesus died on the cross for all your sins. When you sincerely ask Him to forgive you, He will do it. The cross brings you forgiveness for all your sins.

Jesus, thank You that You forgive me all my sins. I come to You, asking you to forgive me for the sins in my life.

Jesus died for you on the cross and forgave you your sins.

READ

Psalm 103:12 — As far as the east is from the west, so far has He removed our transgressions from us.

❓ The Bible uses another image for what the Lord does with your sins when you ask Him to forgive you. What is it?

(Hint: Micah 7:19)

ANSWER: He hurls it into the depths of the sea

God wants you to believe in Jesus

In the world of today one must work very hard to get anywhere. There are few jobs available, so one must do well at school and university in order to get a good job. On the sporting field the competition is equally severe. Children spend hour after hour and afternoon upon afternoon practising to be the best. You must run the 100 m in less than a certain time before you can get provincial colours. In matric your percentage must be above a certain level in order to get a study bursary.

Perhaps you are already getting anxious about everything that needs to be done in your life. There is nothing that does not require hard work. I have good news for you: God tells us in John 1:12 that to become his child, you only have to believe in Jesus. This means that you must accept Jesus as your Saviour. You must realise that what Jesus did for you on the cross, is the gift He offers you. This gift is God's love and grace. All you have to do is to accept this gift by giving your whole life to Jesus.

> Jesus, thank You for dying on the cross for my sins. I choose to believe in You and to accept You as my Saviour.

By believing in Jesus – that means to accept Him as your Saviour – you become God's child.

READ

John 3:36 – Whoever believes in the Son has eternal life, but whoever rejects the Son will not see life, for God's wrath remains on him.

Deeds must follow after faith, the Bible tells us in James 2:17 and 26. Write down a few deeds that, according to you, should flow from your faith in Jesus:

God's gift to you is eternal life

Joanna was celebrating her eleventh birthday. She wished that her grandfather and grandmother could be present. She hadn't seen them for a long time and she was longing for her beloved grandmother and grandfather. She would have to wait until the December holidays to see them again. Early that morning her father, mother and two brothers came to her room to sing to her. Everybody was sitting on her bed and she was very excited while she was opening her presents. She was glad about everything she received and was handing out hugs. Suddenly the doorbell rang. Her father told her to open the door. She ran to the door, opened it … and her grandmother and grandfather were standing in the doorway. She shouted for joy and started to cry. "Oh, this is the biggest present of all!"

Jesus died on the cross for you and me. God loves you so much that He let Jesus die in your place. The very good news is that when you and I become children of God, God gives us eternal life as a gift. It is not something that we have to earn. It is God's gift to his children. In 2 Peter 3:15 we read that He wants everyone to give his or her life to Jesus, so that everyone can receive the biggest gift of all: to live eternally with God in heaven. Have you accepted this gift yet?

Lord, thank You for the most wonderful gift of all times. Thank You that I may belong to You and that my life is in your hands.

God gives you eternal life as a gift.

READ

1 John 5:12 -- He who has the Son has life; he who does not have the Son of God does not have life.

Jesus calls heaven a home. What kind of home is He talking about?

(Hint: John 14:2)

ANSWER: The house of God, his Father

God wants you to be certain that you are going to heaven

There are so many things people wonder about and hope for nowadays. Many people wonder whether they would still have a job tomorrow. Other's friends are nasty to them all the time and they wonder whether they would still have friends. Some people hope that they will do well in the examination, even though they have not worked very hard. Others hope that the weather will get better before they go on holiday. Sometimes you wonder what you are going to get for Christmas or for your birthday. There is one thing, however, that God doesn't want you to have any doubts about, something which you mustn't just hope for, but be sure of: where you are going when you die. This is the one thing of which you can and must be certain.

1 John 5:13 clearly tells us that God wants us to be 100% certain that we have eternal life. That is what we call being secure in our faith. God wants you to be sure of your faith. It is one thing you shouldn't wonder about nor just hope for. Where you will be after death, is too important to be uncertain about. That is why God wants you to make sure of your eternal destination. Have you given your life to Jesus yet? Have you accepted Jesus as your Saviour? Only then can you be 100% certain that you have the Son. And whoever has the Son, has eternal life.

Lord, I give You my whole life. Thank You, Jesus, for being my Saviour. Thank You that I may now be certain that I am a child of God.

God wants you to be certain that, should you die now, you will live with Jesus in heaven for ever.

READ

1 John 5:13 – I write these things to you who believe in the name of the Son of God so that you may know that you have eternal life.

? Who gave his whole life to Jesus on the way to Damascus?

(Hint: Acts 9:19-20)

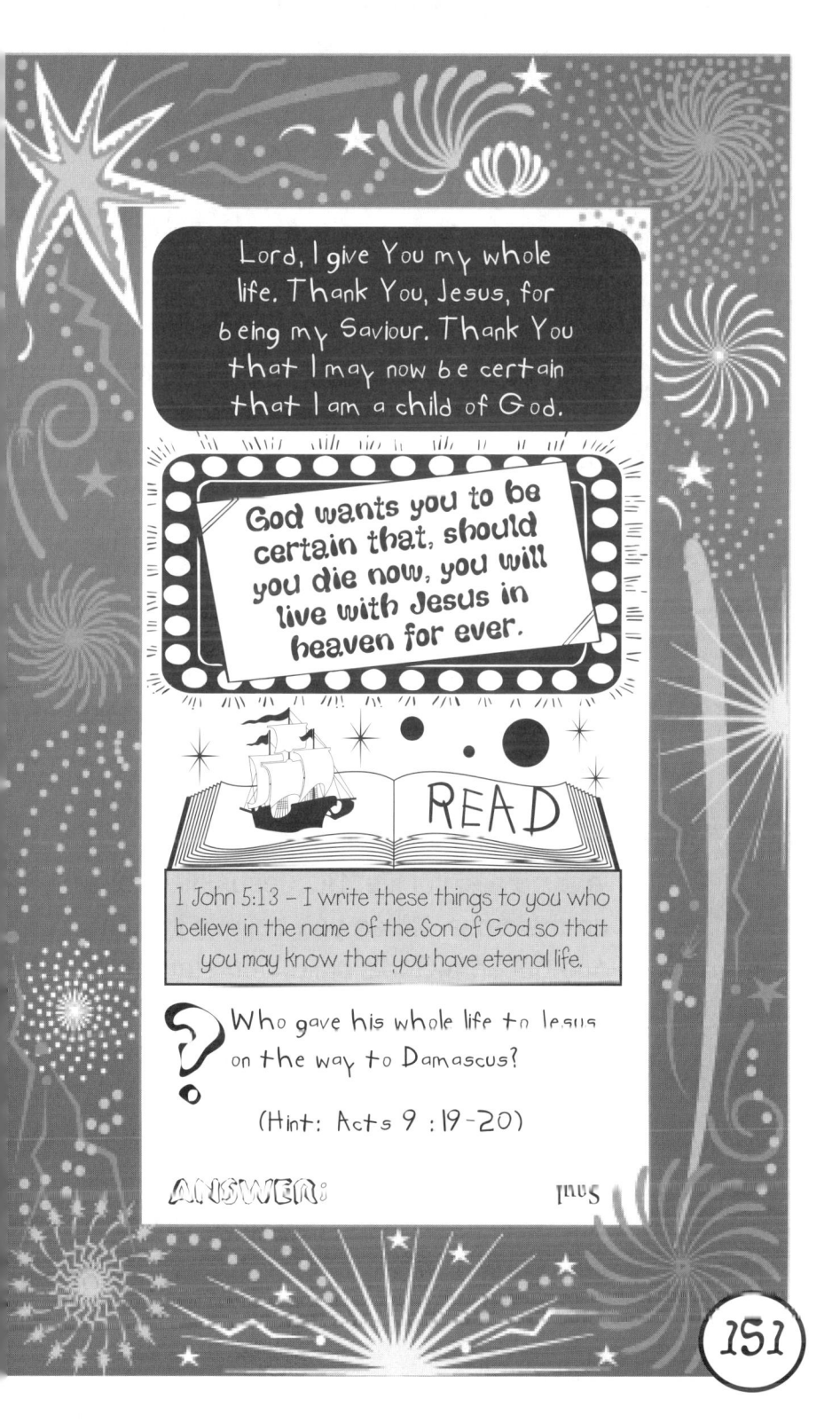

ANSWER: Paul

Jesus makes you brand-new

Lee-Anne's mother was feeling despondent and complained to her husband, "John, just look at the lounge furniture. It is falling apart. Can't I take it to an upholsterer to have it redone? I won't pick the most expensive material. Please?" So the lounge suite was taken to the upholsterers and a week later Lee-Anne couldn't believe her eyes. "Mum, it can't be the same suite! It looks brand-new."

This is precisely what Jesus did for you and me on the cross. We are sinners leading a sinful life. But Jesus died for us on the cross. When you believe in Him and become God's child, you start a brand-new life. In 2 Corinthians 5:17 the Bible tells you that when you belong to Jesus, you are a new person. Jesus makes you a new person – someone who has been forgiven and delivered from all sin. Now you can continue your life as a new person.

Jesus, thank You that your death on the cross has made me brand-new. Thank You for forgiving me and delivering me from all my sins.

Jesus forgives you for and delivers you from all your sins and so makes you a brand-new person.

READ

Revelation 21:5 – He who was seated on the throne said, "I am making everything new!"

Read Ephesians 4:25-32 and write down a few characteristics of the life of a new-born person.

God loved you first

In class your teacher regularly asks questions and then your hands shoot up in the air almost at the same time. Then the poor teacher has to decide whose hand was in the air first. And time and again somebody is unhappy, because he believes that his hand was up first.

When you tell the Lord that you love Him and that you want to live for Him with all your heart, there is one thing you can be sure of: God loved you first. 1 John 4:19 describes it very well. God didn't wait for you to love him first. No, God took the first step. Now you can react by loving Him. And God showed his love for you by letting Jesus die for you on the cross.

What is your reaction to God's act of love? Does your whole life belong to Jesus and are you God's child who live for Him only because He loved you first?

Lord, thank You that You loved me first. I now give You my whole life and choose to love You.

God loved you first and showed it by letting Jesus die on the cross for your sins.

READ

1 John 4:19 – We love because He first loved us.

In the space below write down what Zephaniah 3:17 tells you about God's feelings for you.

Only the blood of Jesus brings forgiveness

In Biblical times God's people sacrificed animals to show how grateful they were for all God had done for them. Whenever they repented, they also sacrificed animals. The high priest then entered the temple's Most Holy Place. There he prayed to God to forgive the sins of his people. Jesus became the High Priest who entered the Most Holy Place for you and me. Jesus, and not goats and heifers, was sacrificed to deliver you and me from our sins.

The Bible teaches us in Hebrews 9:12 that it was the blood of Jesus that gave us eternal redemption (made us forever free from sin). Never again will it be necessary to sacrifice an animal for man's sins. Jesus walked that road for you and for me. Jesus is the Lamb of God who died on the cross to deliver you and me for all eternity. Is the Lamb of God your King and eternal Saviour?

Jesus, thank You for delivering me with your blood for all eternity. Thank You for being the Lamb of God who was sacrificed for me.

Through his blood on the cross, Jesus obtained forgiveness for you.

READ

Hebrews 9:28 – So Christ was sacrificed once to take away the sins of many people.

What did the Lord provide when Abraham went to sacrifice his son in obedience to God?

(Hint: Genesis 22:13)

ANSWER: A ram caught by its horns

We can't buy or earn forgiveness

We can buy almost everything nowadays if we have money. If you want a Sony play station, all you have to do is to ask your mum or dad or save for it yourself. But the fact remains that you can buy it. Most people spend years saving for a beautiful house or a luxurious car. Some are lucky enough to get company cars. They love driving around in them and enjoy the luxury of them. Or you can go on a lovely, very expensive holiday. You can even go skiing in the Swiss Alps or visit Wimbledon in England.

But there is one thing that can't be bought or earned: God's mercy or his forgiveness of our sins. We can't save for these things. And no-one else can earn them for you.

1 Peter 1:18-19 says that all the gold and silver cannot redeem you from your empty way of life. It was Jesus' suffering and blood alone that did this. Have you accepted this and made Jesus the King of your life?

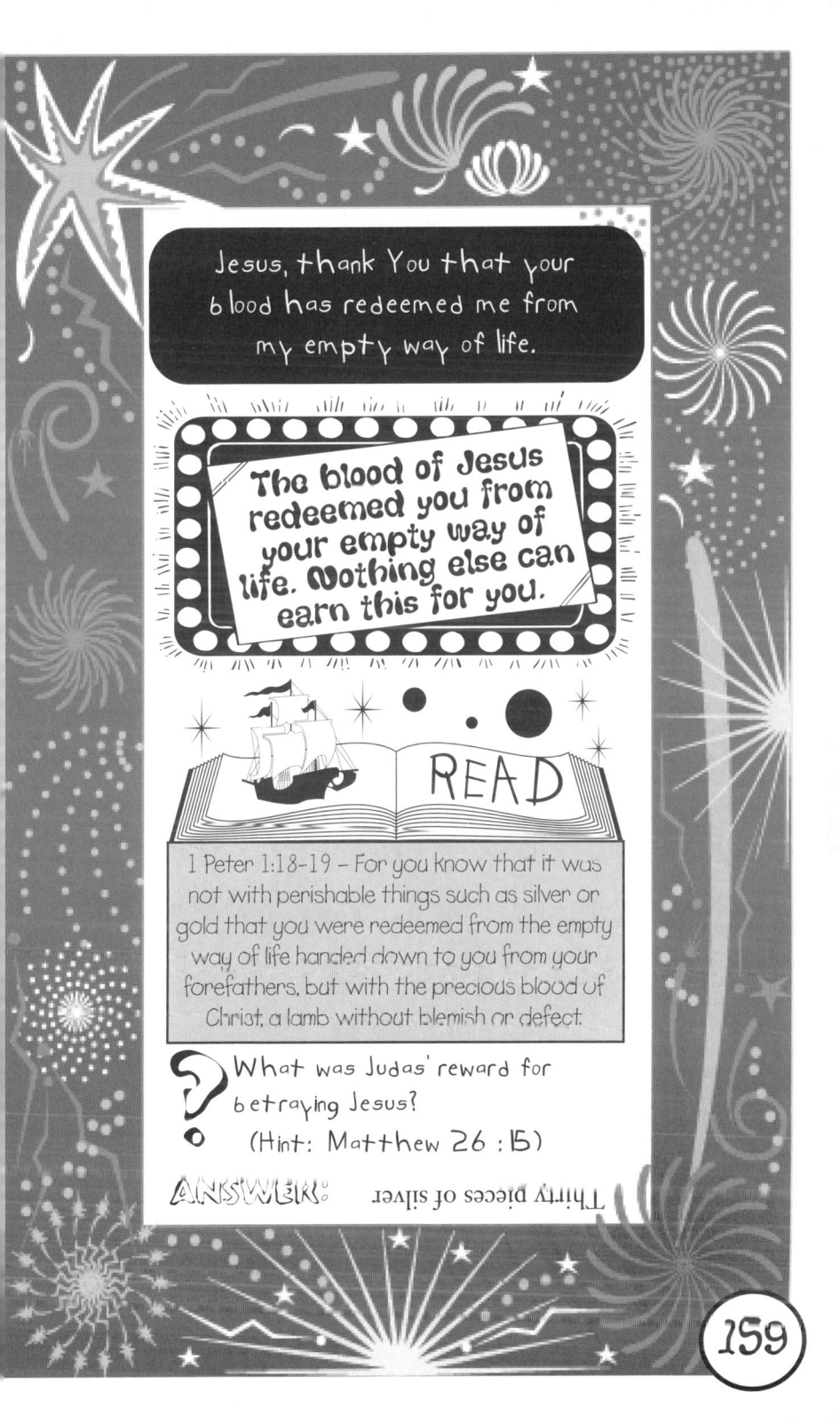

Jesus, thank You that Your blood has redeemed me from my empty way of life.

The blood of Jesus redeemed you from your empty way of life. Nothing else can earn this for you.

READ

1 Peter 1:18-19 – For you know that it was not with perishable things such as silver or gold that you were redeemed from the empty way of life handed down to you from your forefathers, but with the precious blood of Christ, a lamb without blemish or defect.

? What was Judas' reward for betraying Jesus?
(Hint: Matthew 26:15)

ANSWER: Thirty pieces of silver.

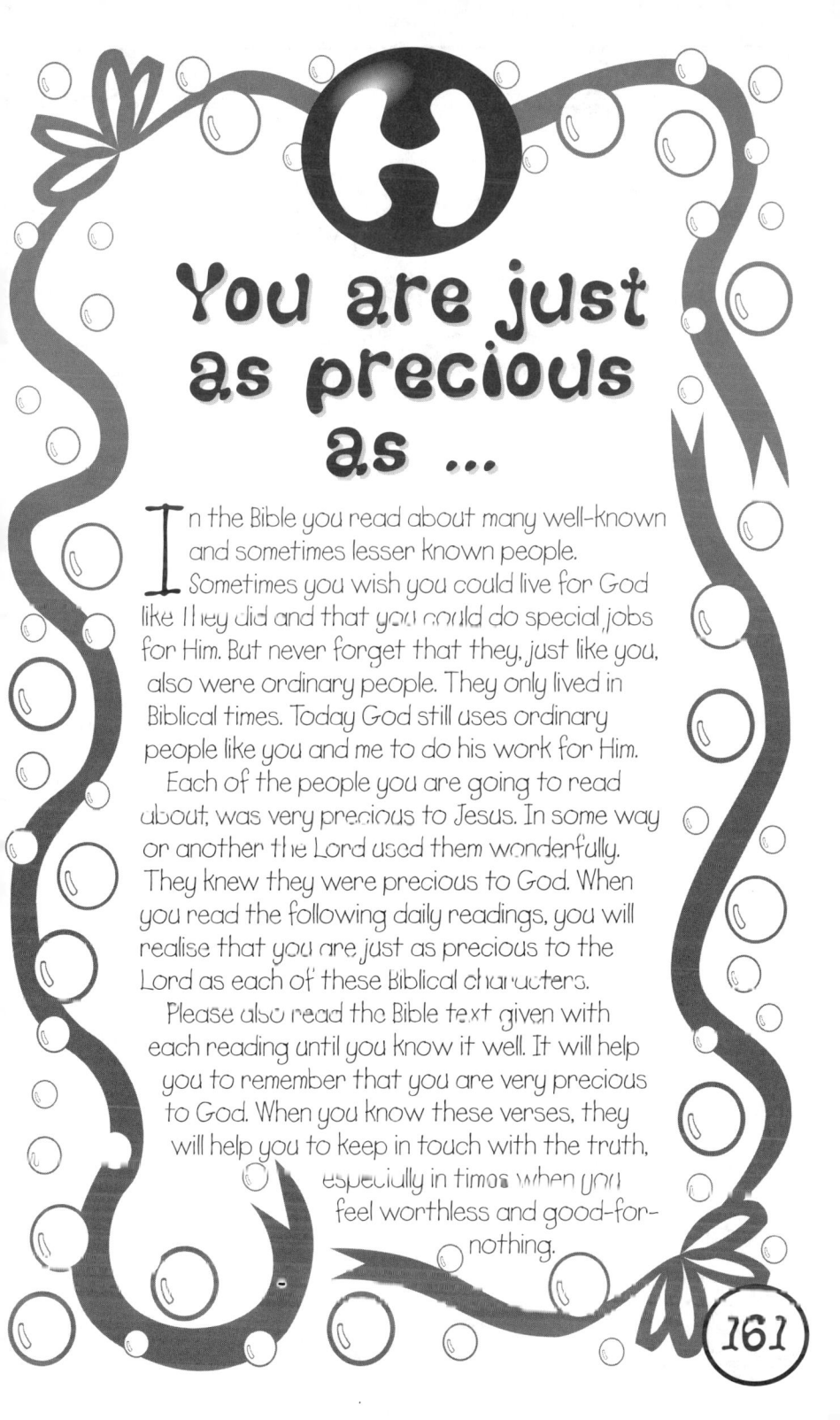

You are just as precious as ...

In the Bible you read about many well-known and sometimes lesser known people. Sometimes you wish you could live for God like they did and that you could do special jobs for Him. But never forget that they, just like you, also were ordinary people. They only lived in Biblical times. Today God still uses ordinary people like you and me to do his work for Him.

Each of the people you are going to read about, was very precious to Jesus. In some way or another the Lord used them wonderfully. They knew they were precious to God. When you read the following daily readings, you will realise that you are just as precious to the Lord as each of these Biblical characters.

Please also read the Bible text given with each reading until you know it well. It will help you to remember that you are very precious to God. When you know these verses, they will help you to keep in touch with the truth, especially in times when you feel worthless and good-for-nothing.

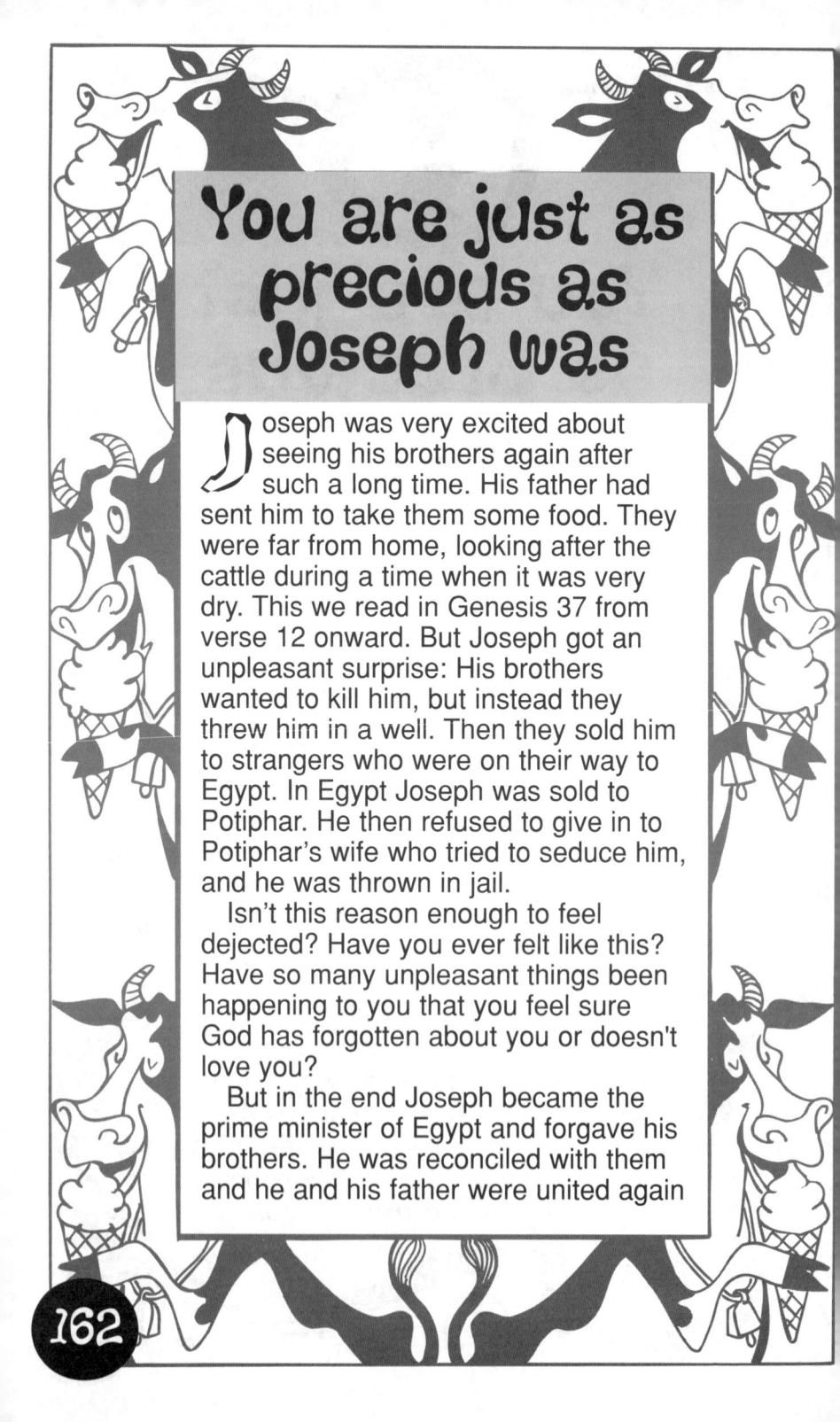

You are just as precious as Joseph was

Joseph was very excited about seeing his brothers again after such a long time. His father had sent him to take them some food. They were far from home, looking after the cattle during a time when it was very dry. This we read in Genesis 37 from verse 12 onward. But Joseph got an unpleasant surprise: His brothers wanted to kill him, but instead they threw him in a well. Then they sold him to strangers who were on their way to Egypt. In Egypt Joseph was sold to Potiphar. He then refused to give in to Potiphar's wife who tried to seduce him, and he was thrown in jail.

Isn't this reason enough to feel dejected? Have you ever felt like this? Have so many unpleasant things been happening to you that you feel sure God has forgotten about you or doesn't love you?

But in the end Joseph became the prime minister of Egypt and forgave his brothers. He was reconciled with them and he and his father were united again

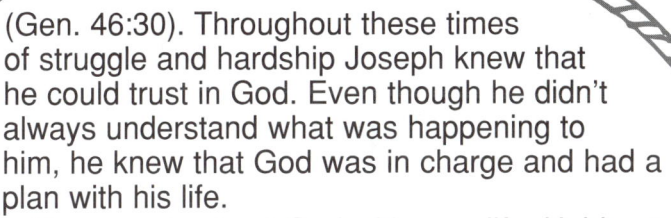

(Gen. 46:30). Throughout these times of struggle and hardship Joseph knew that he could trust in God. Even though he didn't always understand what was happening to him, he knew that God was in charge and had a plan with his life.

You can also trust God with your life. Hold onto Him when bad things that you don't understand, happen to you. Always know that God has a plan with your life, because to Him you are just as precious as Joseph was.

God has a plan with your life.

Lord, thank You that I may know that You have a plan with my life. Thank You that You hold me close to you when I am going through a hard time.

READ

Genesis 39:2 – The Lord was with Joseph and he prospered.

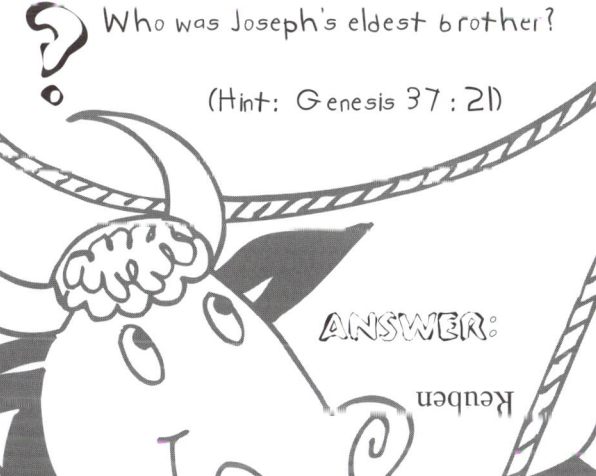

Who was Joseph's eldest brother?

(Hint: Genesis 37:21)

ANSWER: Reuben

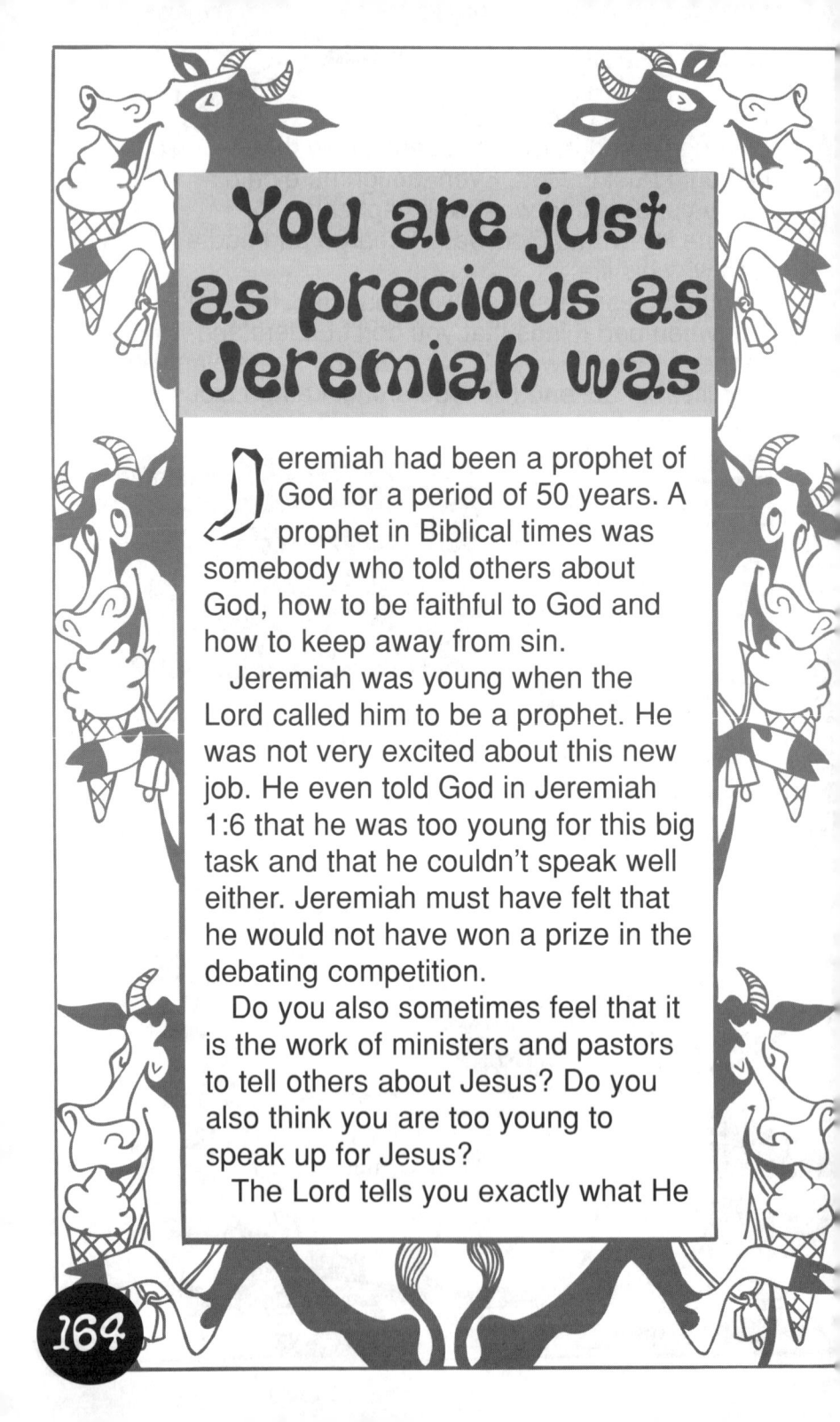

You are just as precious as Jeremiah was

Jeremiah had been a prophet of God for a period of 50 years. A prophet in Biblical times was somebody who told others about God, how to be faithful to God and how to keep away from sin.

Jeremiah was young when the Lord called him to be a prophet. He was not very excited about this new job. He even told God in Jeremiah 1:6 that he was too young for this big task and that he couldn't speak well either. Jeremiah must have felt that he would not have won a prize in the debating competition.

Do you also sometimes feel that it is the work of ministers and pastors to tell others about Jesus? Do you also think you are too young to speak up for Jesus?

The Lord tells you exactly what He

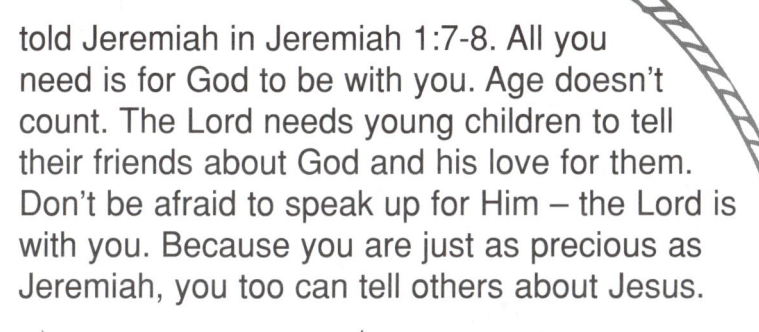

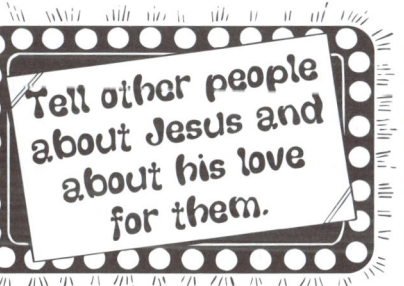

told Jeremiah in Jeremiah 1:7-8. All you need is for God to be with you. Age doesn't count. The Lord needs young children to tell their friends about God and his love for them. Don't be afraid to speak up for Him – the Lord is with you. Because you are just as precious as Jeremiah, you too can tell others about Jesus.

Tell other people about Jesus and about his love for them.

Lord, thank You that You are always with me. Thank You for calling me to tell others about Jesus.

READ

Jeremiah 1:8 – Do not be afraid of them, for I am with you.

The same thing that had happened to Joseph also happened to Jeremiah. What was this?

(Hint: Jeremiah 38:6)

ANSWER: Jeremiah was also thrown into a well

You are just as precious as Noah was

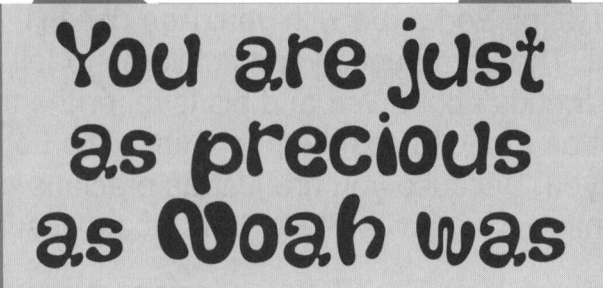

God made man without sin, but Adam and Eve chose against God. In Genesis 6:6 we read that from that time on, God was very unhappy about the sins of man. So God decided to flood the earth with water in order to get rid of the people and their sins.

It was during this time that God called upon Noah to build an ark. Noah was a man who loved God very much and who lived close to Him. Noah was always faithful to the Lord. The Lord spared Noah's life and those of his wife and children. They, together with a male and female of each kind of animal, had to get into the ark before the great flood.

Some of the people who were

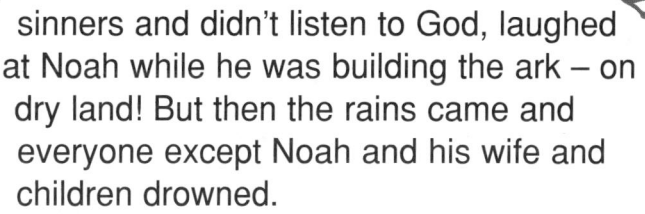

sinners and didn't listen to God, laughed at Noah while he was building the ark – on dry land! But then the rains came and everyone except Noah and his wife and children drowned.

Because you are just as precious to God as Noah, He wants you to be faithful to Him all the time. If you are faithful to God, He will bless you.

Always be faithful to God and you will see how He blesses you.

Lord, help me to be faithful to You all the time. Thank You for looking after me like You looked after Noah.

READ

Genesis 6:9 – Noah was a righteous man, blameless among the people of his time, and he walked with God.

How long did the big flood in Noah's time last? (Hint: Genesis 7:24)

ANSWER:

150 days

167

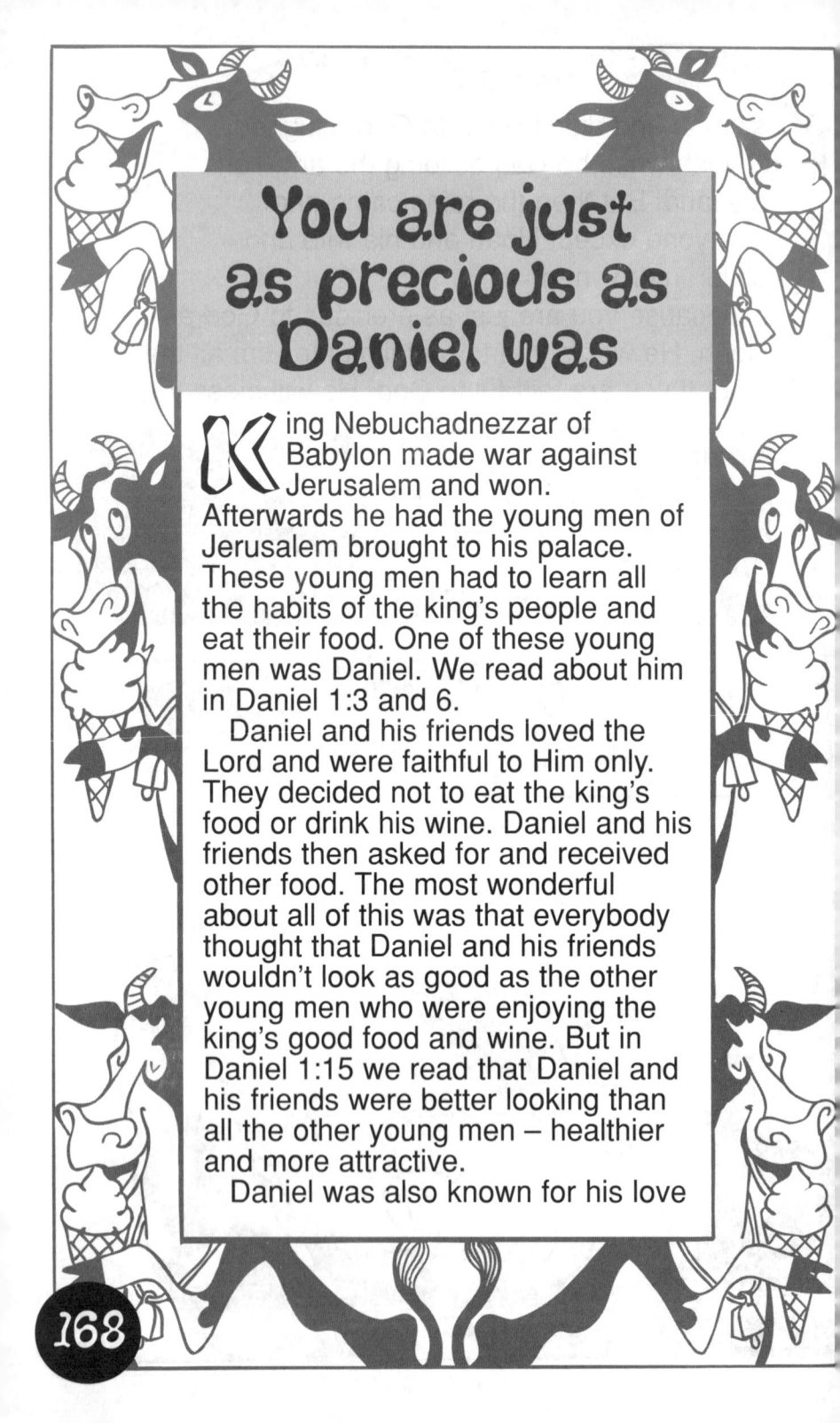

You are just as precious as Daniel was

King Nebuchadnezzar of Babylon made war against Jerusalem and won. Afterwards he had the young men of Jerusalem brought to his palace. These young men had to learn all the habits of the king's people and eat their food. One of these young men was Daniel. We read about him in Daniel 1:3 and 6.

Daniel and his friends loved the Lord and were faithful to Him only. They decided not to eat the king's food or drink his wine. Daniel and his friends then asked for and received other food. The most wonderful about all of this was that everybody thought that Daniel and his friends wouldn't look as good as the other young men who were enjoying the king's good food and wine. But in Daniel 1:15 we read that Daniel and his friends were better looking than all the other young men – healthier and more attractive.

Daniel was also known for his love

for God. He worshipped Him openly and lived for Him (Daniel 6:11).

It was this love for God that resulted in Daniel being thrown into the lions' den. But God shut the lions' mouths and Daniel came out of the den unscathed.

You are just as precious to God as Daniel was. That is why God wants you never to be ashamed of Him. God wants you to be faithful to Him and to tell others about Him.

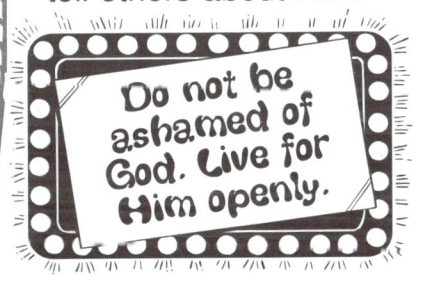

> Do not be ashamed of God. Live for Him openly.

> Lord, like Daniel, I choose not to be ashamed of You. Help me to live in such a way that everyone can see how much I love You.

READ

Psalm 91:11 – For He will command his angels concerning you to guard you in all your ways.

Daniel was thrown in jail because of his faith in God. What did King Nebuchadnezzar do with Daniel's three friends Shadrach, Meshach and Abednego?

(Hint: Daniel 9:20)

ANSWER: They were thrown into a burning oven

You are just as precious as David was

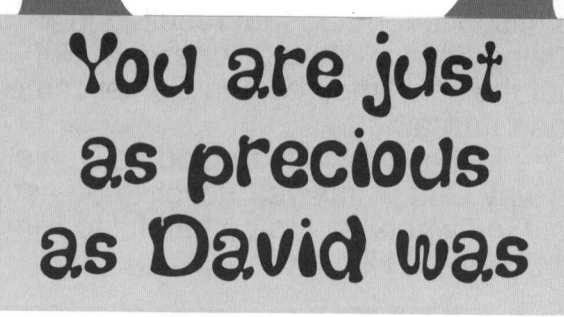

The Lord was disappointed in Saul because he had rejected the Word of the Lord. So it became time to choose a new king for Israel. Samuel had the privilege of anointing the new king. The Lord told Samuel to go to Jesse, because one of his sons would be the new king. We read this story in 1 Samuel 16:1-13.

Samuel looked over Jesse's sons one by one. They were all very handsome. The Lord had given Samuel clear instructions not to look at the boys' outward appearances, for God looked at how they were on the inside. God looks at your heart, not at your looks, how fast you can run or how clever you are. When Samuel couldn't make a choice, he summoned the only child of Jesse who was left – David. David was a shepherd and the youngest of all Jesse's sons. But in spite of that, God decided that he would be the next king of Israel.

Perhaps you consider yourself too young or not good enough to do something for God, because you are not good at sport or schoolwork. Remember: you are just as precious to God as David was and He looks at the way you are on the inside.

God looks at how you are on the inside.

Lord, thank You that I need not excel in order to be good enough for You. Thank You that You look at how I am on the inside.

READ

1 Samuel 16:7b – The Lord does not look at the things man looks at. Man looks at the outward appearance, but the Lord looks at the heart.

Who wanted to kill David?

(Hint: 1 Samuel 18:11)

ANSWER: Saul

You are just as precious as Gideon was

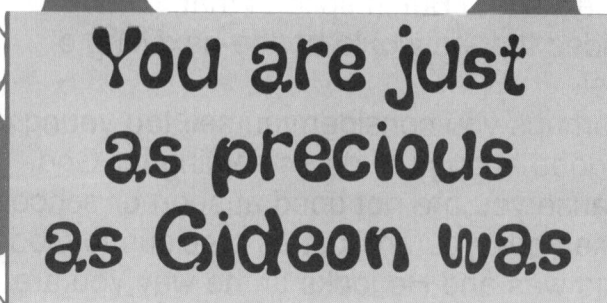

The Israelites started doing evil things again and they hurt God deeply. So God gave them into the hands of the Midianites. The Midianites were a cruel nation who killed the cattle of the Israelites and set fire to their fields. (Judges 6, from verse 1.)

But the Israelites said that they were sorry about what they had done and they showed God that they were really sorry. So the Lord chose Gideon to liberate the Israelites from the hands of the cruel Midianites. But Gideon didn't want to go, because he thought that he was not good enough. He had various excuses, for instance that his family was very poor and that he was the least important of all his brothers and sisters. Sometimes you also feel like this: poor, stupid and unimportant. Then God told

Gideon in Judges 6:16 that He was on Gideon's side, so he was going to beat the Midianites.

This is how you too can know that you are a winner. You belong to Christ, don't you? You and God are always in the majority. You are just as precious to God as Gideon was – that is why you can know that you are very special to Him.

With God on your side you are a winner.

Lord, thank You that You are always with me. Thank you that I can know that I am very special to You.

READ

Psalm 28:7 – The Lord is my strength and my shield; my heart trusts in Him.

Against how many Midianites did Gideon have to fight?

(Hint: Judges 7:12)

ANSWER: They were as many as locusts and the sand on the seashore.

You are just as precious as Asa was

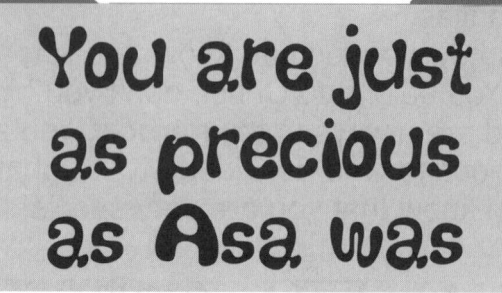

David was an ancestor of Asa. Just like David, Asa loved the Lord very much and was faithful to the Lord all through his life. We read this in 1 Kings 15 from verse 9 onward. Asa was very brave and was king of Jerusalem for 41 years. During the time of his reign, he built many cities and did many brave things. Apart from being king, he was his people's hero.

Today there are also many heroes, for example well-known rugby players, tennis players and singers. They are the idols of young people because they are good at sport or can sing well. Asa, however, was a hero because he loved the Lord and followed Him. What good does it do if you are good at sport or excel in school, but you do not serve the Lord? What good does it do to be everybody's hero, but you are not on your way to heaven?

You must be a hero in God's eyes. You must be a hero because you are faithful to God. You must also look up to other people who love God. There are many sports stars like André Venter, Elana Meyer, Penny Heyns and Jonty Rhodes who live for Jesus with all their hearts. Follow their example.

> A hero in God's eyes is someone who lives for Him with all his heart.

Lord, help me to live in such a way that people don't notice me because I do well, but because I live for You with all my heart.

READ

1 Kings 15:11 – Asa did what was right in the eyes of the Lord, as his father David had done.

Who succeeded Asa as king?

(Hint: 1 Kings 15:24)

ANSWER: Jehoshaphat

You are just as precious as Samuel was

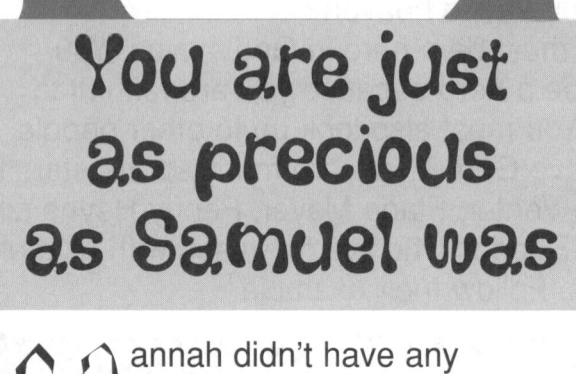

Hannah didn't have any children and many of the other women teased her about it. She was very unhappy and poured out her heart to God. She promised the Lord that, if He gave her a son, she would return this son to Him to serve Him for as long as he lived. We read this in 1 Samuel 1:11. So the Lord blessed Hannah with a son. She called him Samuel, which means "asked from the Lord". Samuel grew up in the temple where God called him to be a prophet. A prophet is someone who tells other people about God.

Each child is a gift from God – whether or not it has been prayed for as was the case with Samuel. God wants each child, whether it is small or not, to serve Him and to be faithful to Him. Many children don't know this and live in sin for a big part of their lives. And sin makes you unhappy.

You are as precious as Samuel was to God. That is why He wants you to be his prophet in your home and among your friends at school and on the sports field.

> God wants you to be his prophet.

> Lord, help me to be your prophet, like Samuel was. Help me to tell others about You.

READ

1 Samuel 3:18 – He is the Lord; let Him do what is good in his eyes.

? Under whose care did Samuel live in the temple?

(Hint: 1 Samuel 3:1)

ANSWER: Eli

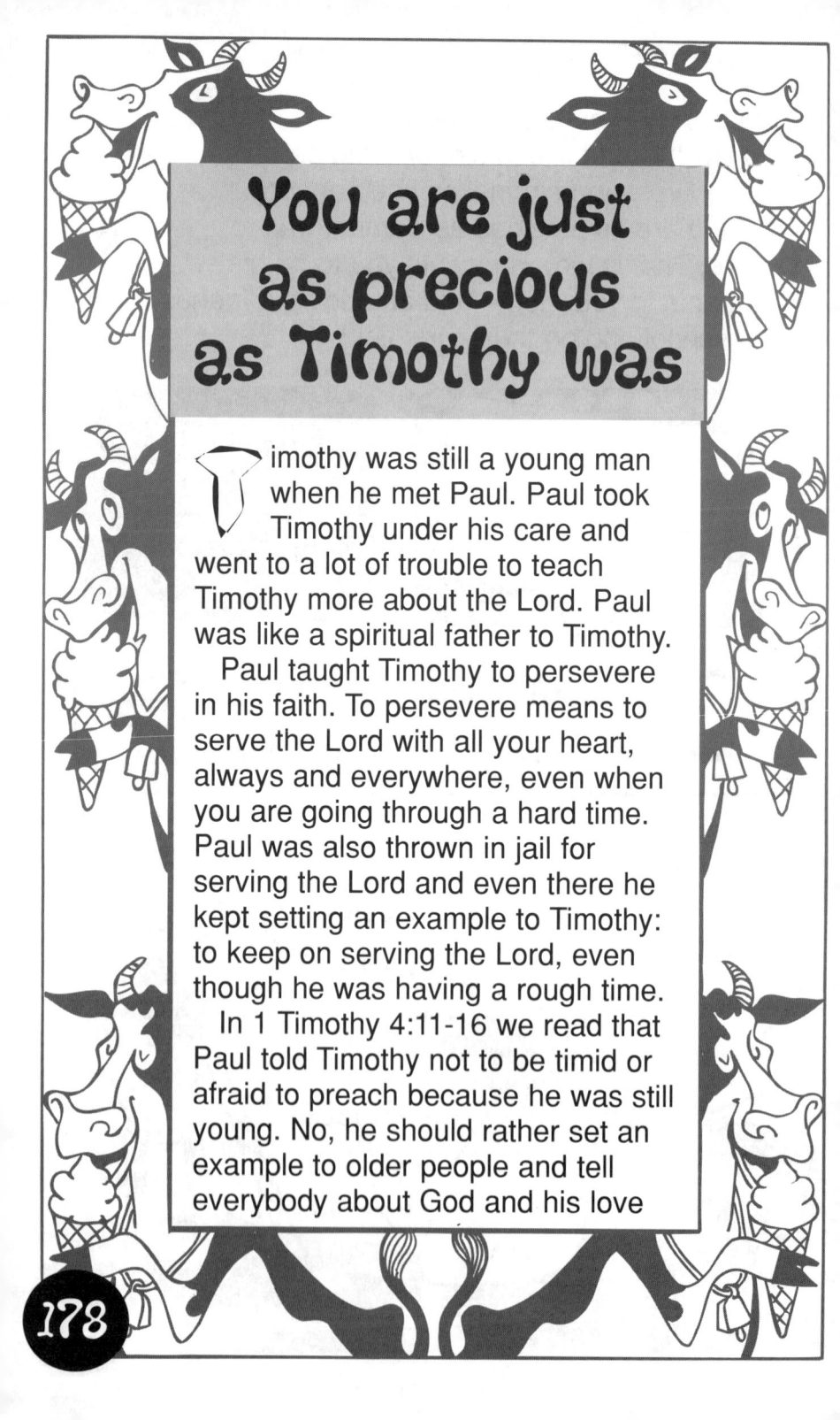

You are just as precious as Timothy was

Timothy was still a young man when he met Paul. Paul took Timothy under his care and went to a lot of trouble to teach Timothy more about the Lord. Paul was like a spiritual father to Timothy.

Paul taught Timothy to persevere in his faith. To persevere means to serve the Lord with all your heart, always and everywhere, even when you are going through a hard time. Paul was also thrown in jail for serving the Lord and even there he kept setting an example to Timothy: to keep on serving the Lord, even though he was having a rough time.

In 1 Timothy 4:11-16 we read that Paul told Timothy not to be timid or afraid to preach because he was still young. No, he should rather set an example to older people and tell everybody about God and his love for them.

You are just as precious to God as Timothy was. That is why God is asking you to set an example to other people, even to older people. Never stop telling people about God and his love.

> God also calls young people to serve Him.

Lord, thank You that I, even though I am young, may set an example to other people. Help me to tell others about You.

READ

1 Timothy 4:7 – Train yourself to be godly.

When will you become an instrument for the Lord to use in his special way?

(Hint: 2 Timothy 2:20)

ANSWER: When you have cleansed yourself from evil – in other words, when you are faithful to God and try your best not to sin any more

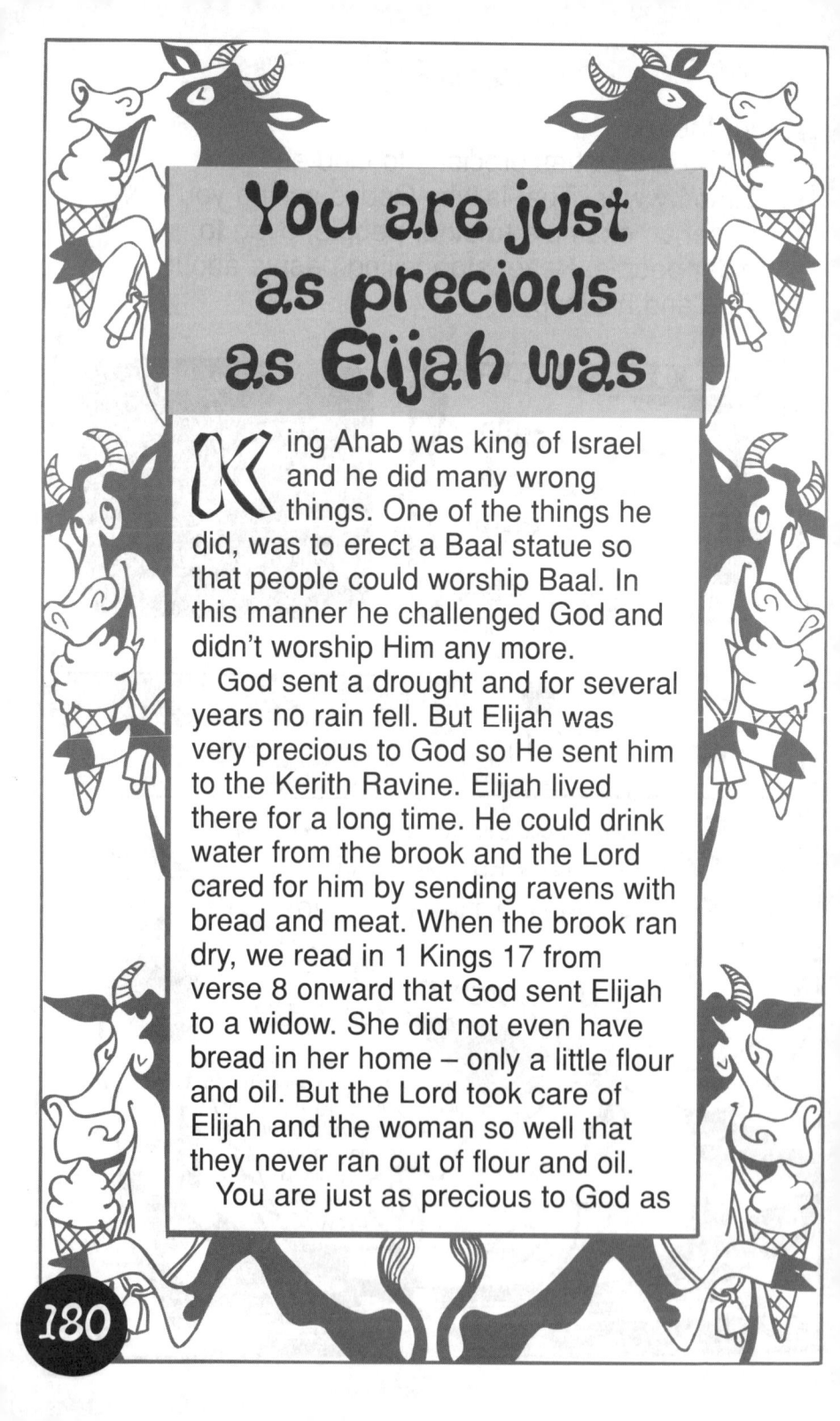

You are just as precious as Elijah was

King Ahab was king of Israel and he did many wrong things. One of the things he did, was to erect a Baal statue so that people could worship Baal. In this manner he challenged God and didn't worship Him any more.

God sent a drought and for several years no rain fell. But Elijah was very precious to God so He sent him to the Kerith Ravine. Elijah lived there for a long time. He could drink water from the brook and the Lord cared for him by sending ravens with bread and meat. When the brook ran dry, we read in 1 Kings 17 from verse 8 onward that God sent Elijah to a widow. She did not even have bread in her home – only a little flour and oil. But the Lord took care of Elijah and the woman so well that they never ran out of flour and oil.

You are just as precious to God as

Elijah was. That is why you needn't worry about anything. Just like the Lord looked after Elijah in a time of drought and little food and water, he will care for you – both in good and in bad times.

God cares for you when times are good and He cares for you when times are bad.

Lord, thank You that I can trust You to take care of me always. Thank you that You will take care of me in bad times too.

READ

Psalm 136:1 – Give thanks to the Lord, for He is good.

What did the widow bake for Elijah?

(Hint: 1 Kings 17:13)

ANSWER: A cake of bread

Promises from God to you

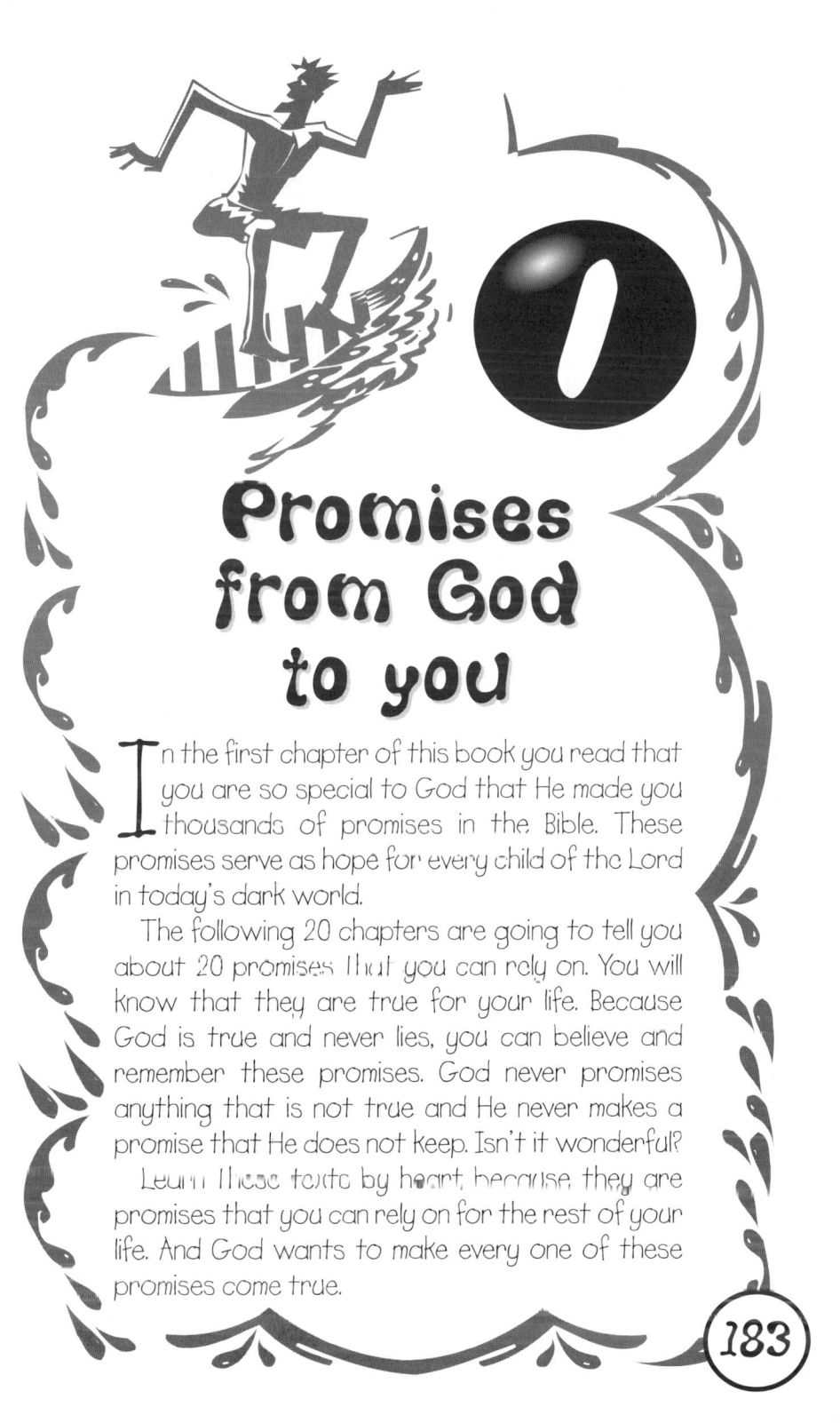

In the first chapter of this book you read that you are so special to God that He made you thousands of promises in the Bible. These promises serve as hope for every child of the Lord in today's dark world.

The following 20 chapters are going to tell you about 20 promises that you can rely on. You will know that they are true for your life. Because God is true and never lies, you can believe and remember these promises. God never promises anything that is not true and He never makes a promise that He does not keep. Isn't it wonderful?

Learn these texts by heart, because they are promises that you can rely on for the rest of your life. And God wants to make every one of these promises come true.

A promise that God's salvation is eternal

Many things in life don't last long. Just think how you enjoyed your birthday parties when you were younger. You looked forward to them for days. You counted these days, and then, too soon, the birthday and the party were over. Or think about a lovely holiday you spent with your family. For weeks you counted the days – then at last it was the first day and you were driving to the seaside. Unfortunately time flies when you are enjoying yourself, and before you knew it, the holiday was over. Nothing lasts for ever – or that is what it seems like.

God gives you the most wonderful promise in the Bible. Hebrews 9:12 tells you that God's salvation is for ever. When He delivers you from your sins, it is for ever. Your salvation cost Him dearly: his Son Jesus had to die on the cross in your place. That is why God's salvation is eternal. Never doubt it.

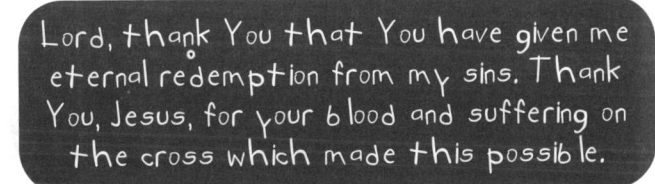

> Lord, thank You that You have given me eternal redemption from my sins. Thank You, Jesus, for your blood and suffering on the cross which made this possible.

God has given me eternal redemption from my sins.

READ

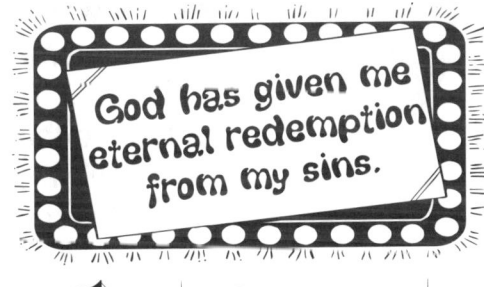

Hebrews 9:12 – He did not enter by means of the blood of goats and calves; but He entered the Most Holy Place once for all by his own blood, having obtained eternal redemption.

? Jesus is also our High Priest. What does that mean?

(Hint: Hebrews 8:3)

ANSWER: A High Priest must have something to sacrifice. Jesus is the Lamb that sacrificed his life for your sins.

185

A promise that God is always with you

Mary was very upset when she came home from school. Her mother tried to comfort her, so that she could tell what had happened. But Mary was heartbroken. At last she calmed down enough to tell her mother that nobody at school wanted to play with her. Nobody came to play with her in the afternoons. Her mother started questioning her carefully. "What about Gertrude, Mary?" Mary replied that she hadn't spoken to Gertrude. "And what about Susan, Mary?" Mary hadn't asked her either. "What about Jessica, Mary?" Mary had also forgotten to ask Jessica. Mary's mother soon realised that Mary hadn't asked anyone to play with her. No wonder they were not playing with her.

You and I sometimes also forget that God would like to be with us. In 2 Chronicles 15:2 He promises that you will find Him if you seek

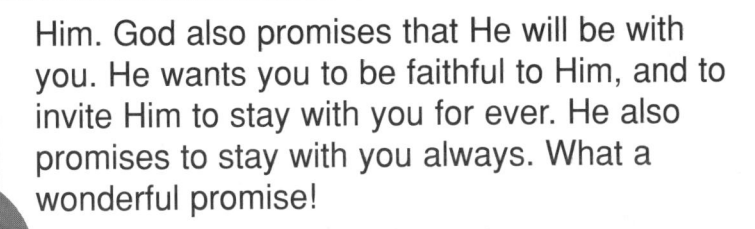

Him. God also promises that He will be with you. He wants you to be faithful to Him, and to invite Him to stay with you for ever. He also promises to stay with you always. What a wonderful promise!

> Lord, thank You that You want to be with me all the time. I now invite You to be with me and to stay with me. Please help me to be faithful to You.

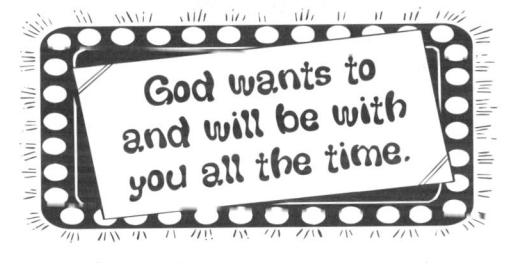

God wants to and will be with you all the time.

READ

2 Chronicles 15:2 – The Lord is with you when you are with Him. If you seek Him, He will be found by you.

? Who killed a lion and a strong Egyptian with only a stick as a weapon? Whose son was he? (Hint: 2 Samuel 23:20-21)

ANSWER: Benaiah, son of Jehoiada

A promise that God hears your prayers and answers them

It was Monday – and for Miss Alice it really felt like a blue Monday. She was standing in front of her grade 5 class and tried her utmost to get them to keep quiet. But today there was great excitement in the grade 5 class of Sunshine Primary School. Because they had collected the largest amount of money with the go-cart event, they could go home earlier that day. For the fifth time Miss Alice shouted, "If you don't keep quiet immediately, I am going to send you out!" For five minutes all went well, but then the children got excited again. Miss Alice sat down on her chair and sighed, "Nobody listens when I talk. And nobody does what I ask."

In Psalm 86:7 God gives you the wonderful promise that He always hears you when you call. And He doesn't only listen. He also answers each prayer. He answers by saying "yes", "no" or "wait a bit". But the truth is, He hears and answers all your prayers.

> Lord, thank You that You hear all my prayers. Thank You that You also answer my prayers. Thank You that I may talk to You any time.

God hears every prayer and answers every one of them.

READ

Psalm 4:3 – Know that the Lord has set apart the godly for himself; the Lord will hear when I call to him

? Who are you worrying about at the moment? Or maybe there are circumstances in your life that trouble you. Write down your prayer below and know that God hears it and will answer.

189

A promise that God is not ashamed of you

As you grow older, you feel embarrassed more easily. You don't like your father or mother to kiss you in front of your friends any more. And, of course, you get so embarrassed when your father or mother wears old-fashioned clothes. You don't want to be seen with them. I am not even talking about your younger brother or sister. They can do the most stupid and crazy things and then you don't know where to hide yourself. Your face turns as red as a beetroot and you are extremely embarrassed. They can be so childish.

God gives you a wonderful promise in Hebrews 11:16. He says He is never ashamed of you. Just think about it: God, the Almighty, the Creator of the heaven and the earth, is never ashamed of you. You, on the other hand, sometimes do things that hurt

God very much – things of which He has the right to be ashamed. No, God is proud of you, because you are his child.

> Lord, thank You that You are never ashamed of me. Please forgive me when I do things that are wrong in your eyes.

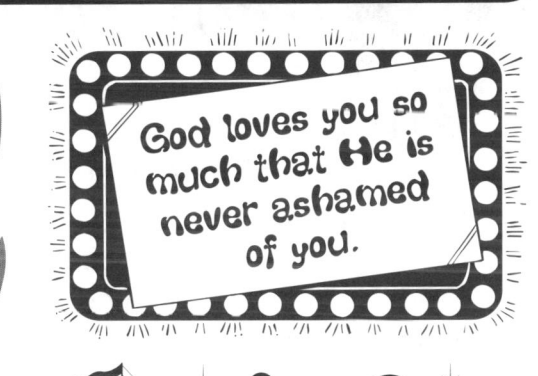

God loves you so much that He is never ashamed of you.

READ

Hebrews 11:16 – Therefore God is not ashamed to be called their God, for He has prepared a city for them.

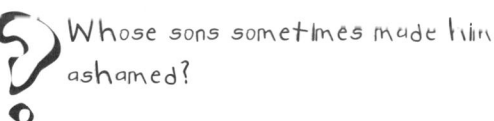

? Whose sons sometimes made him ashamed?

(Hint: 1 Samuel 2:22-24)

ANSWER: Eli

A promise that nothing can separate you from God's love

Rosanne and Freda lived in the beautiful Boland and were best friends. They were together all the time. Sometimes they played at Rosanne's house, sometimes at Freda's. Everyone at school knew that they were very good friends. One day Rosanne came home crying. Her mother listened patiently while Rosanne told her that Freda and her family were moving to Gauteng. Freda's father had been transferred. Freda was very sad, because she might never see her best friend again.

The Lord promises you in Romans 8:38-39 that nothing can separate you from his love. Nothing can make you lose God's love. The Bible here mentions many things that will not make God's love for you come to an end. God's love is everywhere and accompanies you wherever you go. No person or bad experience can take his love away from you. What a fantastic promise to hold onto all the time – especially when you are going through a difficult time.

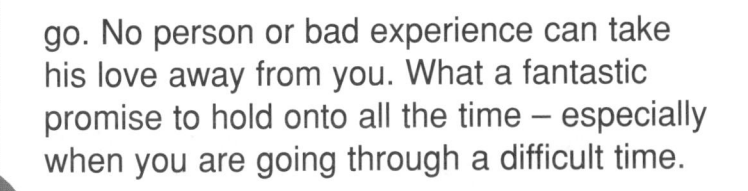

> Lord, thank You for your eternal love. Thank You that absolutely nothing will separate me from your wonderful love.

Nothing, no powers or people or anything else, can separate you from the wonderful love of God.

READ

Romans 8:38 – (Nothing) will be able to separate us from the love of God that is in Christ Jesus our Lord.

Write down below those things that can't separate you from the love of God. (Romans 8:38-39)

A promise that God gives you hope

A few weeks ago I was sitting in a coffee-shop having the most delicious cup of coffee and a piece of chocolate cake. Sitting next to me were two men who were unbelievably negative about life. One of them was complaining about everything that had become so expensive. The other added that, apart from being so expensive, the quality of everything had gone down too. "Yes," the first one said, "and the pollution of the world is terrible and there isn't work for all the people." The second man had to outdo his friend, and said, "Yes, it is a hopeless case." His friend agreed wholeheartedly, "Yes, there definitely is no hope at all."

The very good news is that God gives you hope. It doesn't matter how bleak your circumstances seem. It doesn't matter how bad the world looks to you. God is not from this world. It is He who gives you hope in this world. Psalm 33:18-19 gives you the promise that the Lord will take care of you and that He will keep you alive, even in a time of famine.

> Lord, thank You that I need never become negative. Thank You that You are looking after me every minute of the day. Thank You for giving me hope in a dark world.

God gives you hope during hard times and in a dark world.

READ

Psalm 71:5-6a – For You have been my hope, O Sovereign Lord, my confidence since my youth. From birth I have relied on You.

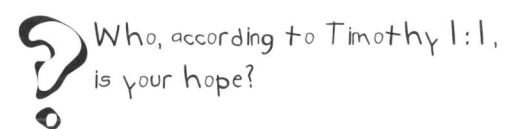

? Who, according to Timothy 1:1, is your hope?

ANSWER: Jesus Christ

A promise that the Word of God will live for ever

Years ago men built a ship called the Titanic. Perhaps you've heard about the film that was made or maybe you have seen it yourself. They planned the ship so carefully that they were sure it would never sink. Never before had such a big ship been built so thoroughly and beautifully. Unfortunately the ship collided with an iceberg in the sea and sank. Hundreds of people died in the tragic accident of this boat that everybody thought would never sink.

In this world there is only one thing that will never die: God's Word. Isaiah 40:8 tells you that the Word of God will live forever. So it is very important that we read it regularly and also learn the Bible texts by heart. This is the only thing that will never die.

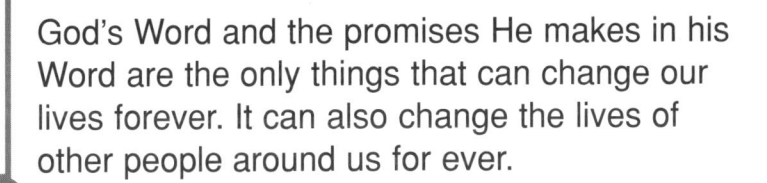

God's Word and the promises He makes in his Word are the only things that can change our lives forever. It can also change the lives of other people around us for ever.

> Lord, thank You for your Word that will never die. Thank You that I can read your Word regularly and that it can change my life forever.

The Word of God will never die.

READ

Matthew 24:35 – Heaven and earth will pass away, but my words will never pass away.

? Many people collect money and possessions as if these things will last forever. What deceitful thing did Jezebel do to get her hands on Naboth's vineyard? (Hint: 1 Kings 21:9-10)

ANSWER: She had Naboth falsely accused and murdered

A promise that your words can make a difference

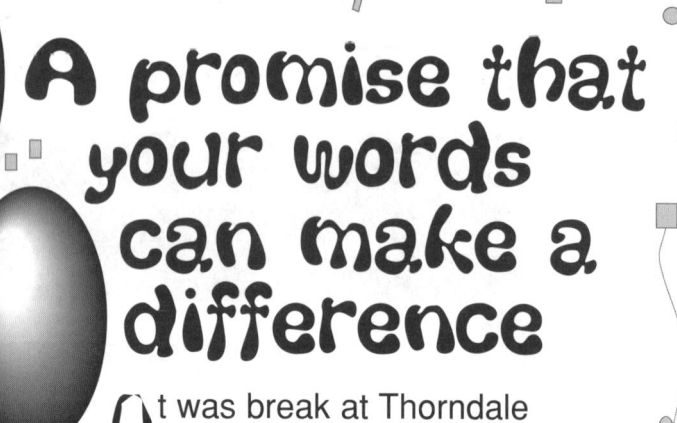

It was break at Thorndale Primary School in the Free State. Peter was making fun of Frank. Mockingly he said, "You failed your test. You're stupid, a real fat-head." Frank was deeply hurt and the next moment he furiously attacked Peter. Everyone could see that a big fight was coming and they ran nearer not to miss anything.

Frank stood in front of Peter with his fists clenched and looked him straight in the eye. "You're a real jellyfish, you half-wit. You're the scum of the earth." Now it was Peter's turn to feel hurt. We see here that the words we utter can hurt deeply.

Proverbs 15:4 teaches us that calm, constructive words can be a blessing to someone else. They can make that person feel better about himself. But we also learn that ugly, insulting and blasphemous words have the power to break someone. Never allow such words to pass over your lips. Only say what is good and beautiful. Your words can make a difference in someone else's life.

> Lord, please help me to choose the words I say to others very carefully, so that I will bless them and not hurt them.

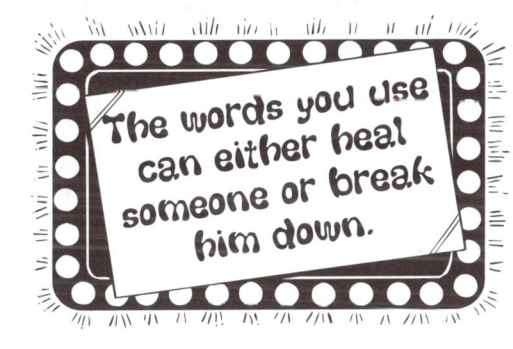

The words you use can either heal someone or break him down.

READ

Proverbs 16:24 - Pleasant words are a honeycomb, sweet to the soul and healing to the bones.

Think of some members of your family and some of your school friends to whom your words can mean something. Write down below what you are going to say to them.

A promise that the Lord will bless you when you speak the truth.

Maritza's mother was having coffee with Mary-Anne's mum. Mary-Anne's mother was talking about the movie Maritza and Mary-Anne had seen the the previous day. Afterwards they had gone to the Wimpy to have a milkshake. Maritza's mother was confused, because Maritza had told her that she and Mary-Anne were going to study for a maths test the next day. When she came home, she told her mother how hard they had studied and that she knew the work. Maritza never thought that her mother would find out that she had lied. She was in deep trouble now. She was going to learn that it doesn't pay to lie.

In 1 Peter 3:10 the Bible

teaches you that, if you want to be really happy and enjoy life, you must never tell lies. The devil is the father of the lie and he wants you to lie.

Remember that God wants you to speak the truth.

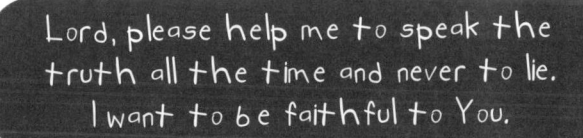

> Lord, please help me to speak the truth all the time and never to lie. I want to be faithful to You.

God wants you to always speak the truth so that He can bless you.

READ

Proverbs 12:19 – Truthful lips endure forever, but a lying tongue lasts only a moment.

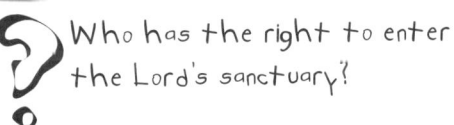

? Who has the right to enter the Lord's sanctuary?

(Hint: Psalm 15 : 1-3)

ANSWER: "He who walks blameless and who does what is righteous, who speaks the truth from his heart and has no slander on his tongue."

A promise that God will bless you if you honour your parents

Like you and your friends, your parents also grow older. They once were just as young as you are now. They have made many mistakes in their lives and have learnt from these mistakes. They care about you, so they set certain boundaries for you. This is where the word "discipline" comes from. You and your friends feel that they don't really understand you and are going out of their way to complicate your lives. What is more, they fuss over you and don't understand modern life. Sometimes you think that they do it on purpose to spite you whenever they can.

Nothing can be further from the truth. Your parents love you. They set boundaries because they care. Children who grow up without discipline are missing out on parents who care about them and love them – and are showing it with rules and discipline.

Ephesians 6:2 promises that God will bless you if you listen to your parents and honour them.

> Lord, please help me to honour my parents and to obey them. Help me to realise that they are strict because they love me and care for me.

When you honour your parents and listen to what they say, God will bless you.

READ

Proverbs 22:6 – Train a child in the way he should go, and when he is old he will not turn from it.

In the space below, write down a few things you can do to show your parents that you appreciate and love them.

A promise that God will bless your compassion

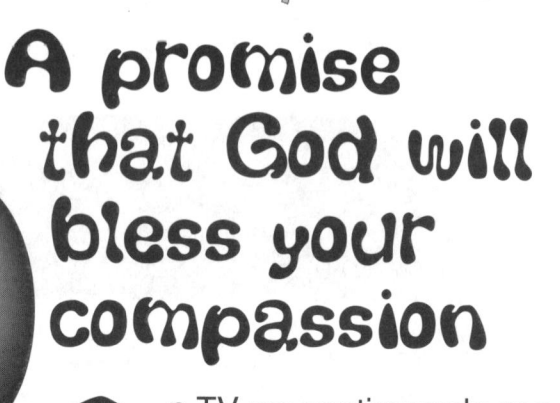

On TV we continuously see scenes of sick and hungry people in Africa who are dying. At night you and I sleep in a nice warm bed while thousands of people in our country don't even have a home. Sometimes you complain about the food at home being boring or not to your taste. Then you forget the millions of children and needy people around you who haven't even had a slice of bread to still their hunger.

To be compassionate means to see the need around you and to do something about it. In Proverbs 28:27 the Lord promises you that when you reach out to people in need, you will never lack anything. Look around you for friends at school who are poor and needy. You and your friends can definitely make a difference to their lives.

> Lord, please help me to watch out for people in need. Help me to make a difference to their situation.

The Lord wants to use you to show compassion to people and He wants to bless you for it.

READ

Psalm 41:1 – Blessed is he who has regard for the weak; the Lord delivers him in times of trouble.

Think of practical things you and your friends can do to help those children at your school who are in need.

A promise that God makes you capable

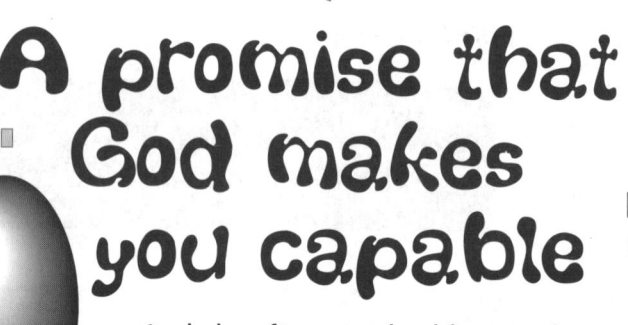

Chris often sat looking at the other children around him in class. He thought they were all so clever, while he was so stupid. During the athletics season he felt like a real tortoise, because everybody could run faster that he could. He couldn't even play rugby, for he couldn't catch a ball. Chris didn't even sing in the choir, because he thought that he had a flat voice. He considered himself to be bad at everything and believed that he could do nothing properly.

What Chris was forgetting, was that each person received a talent from God. Yes, all our talents come from Him. Nothing is ours. That is why we should not brag when we have done something well, because it is God who gave us the talent to do it.

In 2 Corinthians 3:5-6 God promises us that He has given

each of us a talent. It is God who enabled you and me to do some things well. We must recognise our talents and develop them to glorify Him.

> Lord, thank You for giving me a talent too. Please help me to develop it to your glory.

God enabled you to do some things better than others. He gave you talents.

READ

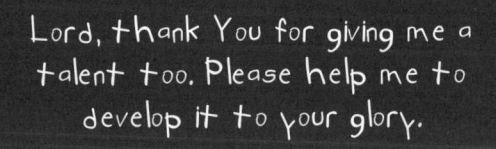

2 Corinthians 3:5 – Not that we are competent in ourselves to claim anything for ourselves, but our competence comes from God.

? What was David's special talent?

(Hint: 1 Samuel 16 : 23)

ANSWER: He could play the harp very well

A promise of peace when you do what is right

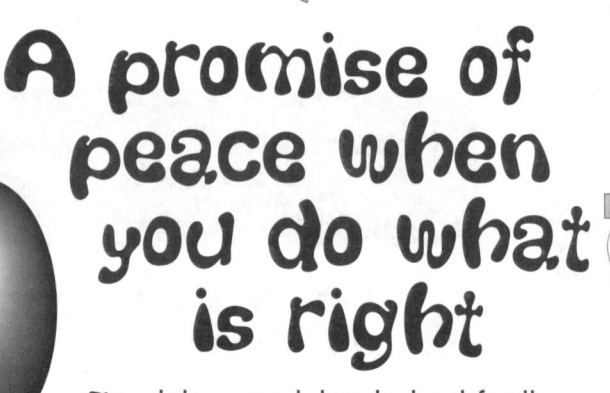

Ricky was lying in bed feeling very bad about himself. At school that day he had put one of his classmates' pencils in his own pocket. The day before he had taken R2 belonging to one of the girls in his class and had spent it at the tuck-shop. Now he was tired of coping with so much tension and turmoil because he was not living as he should.

Geraldine, on the other hand, copied the work of one of her friends while they were writing a maths test. Now she was also sitting in her room, feeling very bad about herself.

You can learn from the mistakes made by Ricky and Geraldine.

In Isaiah 32:17 the Lord promises that if you do the right thing, He will grant you peace. He encourages you to do the right thing, because then you'll have peace in your heart. To do the right thing is to keep away from what is wrong and to be faithful only to God. When you live like this, you will experience God's peace.

> Lord, please help me to do the right thing all the time, so that I may experience your peace.

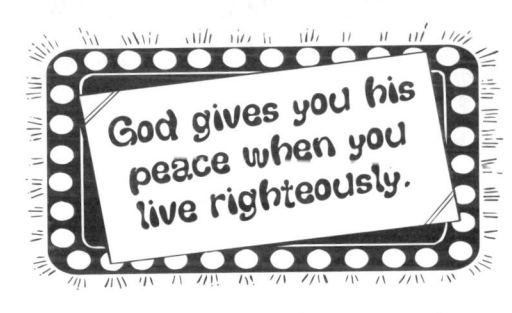

God gives you his peace when you live righteously.

READ

Isaiah 32:17 – The fruit of righteousness will be peace; the effect of righteousness will be quietness and confidence for ever.

? What does the Bible call someone who makes unholy plans and is untrustworthy – someone who doesn't do what is right?
(Hint: Isaiah 32:7)

ANSWER: A scoundrel

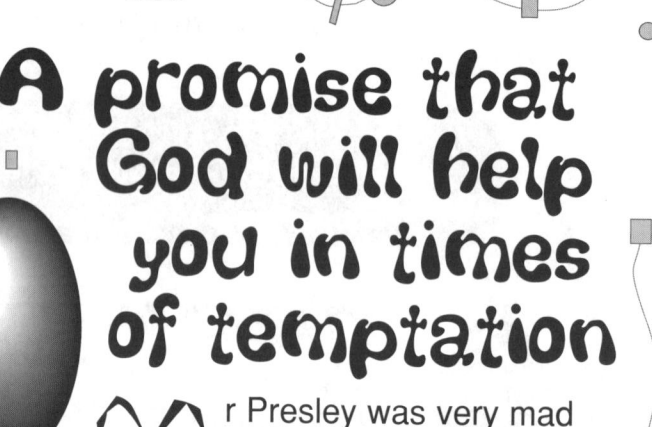

A promise that God will help you in times of temptation

Mr Presley was very mad at Squirrels. During break Squirrels had said very mean things to Susan, like her being a pain in the back. Squirrels explained to Mr Presley that he couldn't help it. Before he knew it, he had already said it. He didn't really want to do it. Mr Presley then told Squirrels about the boy who took a packet of sweets from the shop "by accident". He put it in his pocket without paying for it. When the shop-owner called the police, the boy explained that he had taken them "by accident", not intentionally. The police didn't believe him. His father was very angry and gave him a terrible hiding.

You see, temptation comes from the devil. He wants you to commit sin. The choice that you make, is not "by accident". No, you choose to do or not to do something.

In 1 Corinthians 10:13 the Lord promises that when temptation crosses your path, He will help you to make the right choice – against sin and for God. So remember to ask God to help you make the right choice in a time of temptation. He promises that He will.

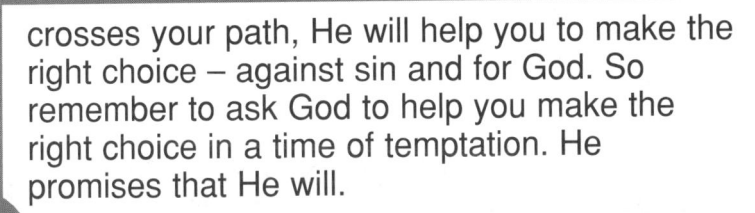

> Lord, when I am tempted, please help me to choose against sin and for You. Thank You that, in a time of temptation, I can know that You are there for me.

When a temptation comes your way, God will help you not to sin.

READ

1 Corinthians 10:13 – He will not let you be tempted beyond what you can bear. But when you are tempted, He will also provide a way out so that you can stand up under it.

Write down on a piece of paper the temptations that cross your path each day. Ask the Lord to help you not to give in to these temptations.

A promise that the Lord determines your future

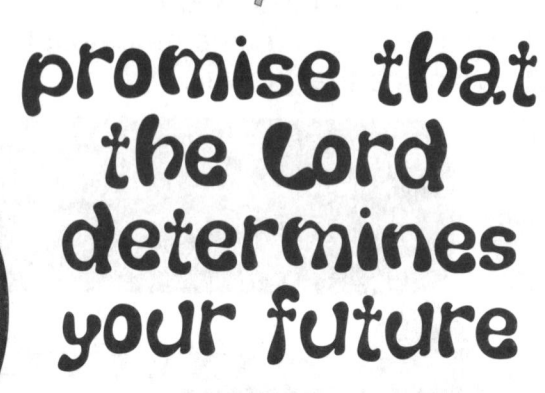

Rolene's father and mother were desperate. Rolene was under great stress. She had to make certain decisions about her future, but she felt that this future was just too bleak. She wanted to take certain subjects in high school, but what if she couldn't find work in that field? What if she couldn't use these subjects to go to university or the technicon? The more her parents tried to calm her, the less success they had. The reason: Rolene had already decided that the future looked bleak.

In Isaiah 42:16 the Lord promises that He can even lead the blind on paths they don't know. He who is God, can make the rough places smooth. So there is no need to worry about your future. Talk to God about everything you do and He will lead you on your future path.

> Lord, thank You that You are also in control of my future. Thank You that I can trust You with my whole heart.

You can trust the Lord with your future, because He determines the way you must go.

READ

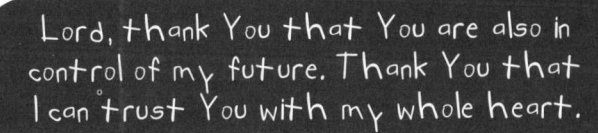

Psalm 32:8 – I will instruct you and teach you in the way you should go. I will counsel you and watch over you.

? The Lord guides you wherever you go. Even if you go in two directions, the Lord will guide you. What are these two directions?

(Hint: Psalm 139 : 9-10)

ANSWER: The east and the west

A promise that the right friends will be a blessing to you

During the past holiday Ryan attended an exciting camp held by their congregation's youth action. On this camp he heard the wonderful news of Jesus and the cross. Ryan gave his life to Jesus and he was very excited, because he knew that he was a new person now. Back at school Ryan started spending time with the wrong friends – friends who did wrong things and exasperated the teachers.

Before long things were not going so well for Ryan. He started forgetting to do his homework. He even started using foul language again and was rude to his family. At last Ryan decided enough was enough and he began taking an active part in his school's Christian activities. There he made new friends who also loved God. From then on he spent wonderful times with these new friends.

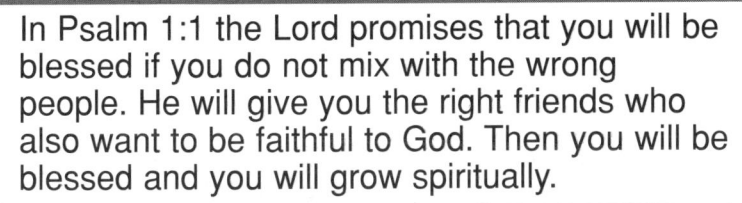

In Psalm 1:1 the Lord promises that you will be blessed if you do not mix with the wrong people. He will give you the right friends who also want to be faithful to God. Then you will be blessed and you will grow spiritually.

> Lord, please help me to choose my friends well. I want to be faithful to You, also in choosing my friends. Thank You that You will bless me when I do so.

The Lord wants to bless you with friends who also love Him.

READ

Proverbs 17:17 – A friends loves at all times, and a brother is born for adversity.

Write down the names of your friends who know God and love him. Make sure that you are a true friend to them.

A promise that God will keep you safe

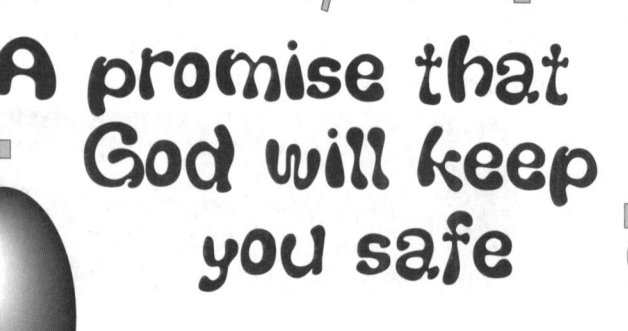

When you watch the news on TV, you get very scared. Newspaper reports are even worse. You hear and read about theft, rape and many different kinds of crime everywhere. Houses are surrounded by high fences or walls and everywhere you look, you see barbed wire. At school, bicycles get stolen and sometimes you hear about strangers abducting children by offering them lifts. Your parents taught you not to get into strangers' cars. You feel unsafe, even in daylight. At night it is much worse.

In Psalm 9:9 the Lord gives you a wonderful promise: The Lord is a stronghold in times of trouble. Yes, it is the Lord who protects you in troubled times and when you are scared. It is God who keeps you safe.

> Lord, thank You for protecting me when I feel insecure. Thank You for being my refuge.

It is the Lord who protects you when you are in danger.

READ

Psalm 46:1 - God is our refuge and strength, an ever-present help in trouble.

? Which man was stoned to death for loving Jesus?

(Hint: Acts 7:55 and 59)

ANSWER: Stephen

A promise of being blessed when you are faithful to God

Katherine had given her life to Jesus. Everybody could see that a huge change had taken place in her life. She didn't use foul language any more or talk unkindly about the other children. When she heard someone swear, Katherine would tell that person not to do so. It was Katherine who sided with a school friend when some of the other children were nasty to her.

One day she was telling one of the children at school not to use dirty language or talk behind other people's backs. The child suddenly got mad and started shouting at Katherine in a nasty and rude way. Katherine felt sad and wondered whether it was worthwhile to live for Jesus with one's whole heart.

God's promise to his children assures us that He will bless us when we are treated badly because of Him. Yes, when you are faithful to the Lord, He will compensate you for it. Especially when you are mocked for being a Christian, as written in Matthew 5:10.

> Lord, thank You that I needn't get upset when other children mock me for standing up for You. Thank You for noticing it and compensating me for it.

The Lord will bless you when you stand up for Him, even though other children make fun of you

READ

1 Peter 4:14 – If you are insulted because of the Name of Christ, you are blessed, for the Spirit of glory and of God rests on you.

Who, according to 1 Corinthians 4:9-13, had been persecuted in Biblical times?

ANSWER: The apostles, of whom Peter was one of the well-known ones.

A promise that God comforts you when you are sad

Little Derek had received the most beautiful dog from his father and mother for his birthday. He looked after him every day, played with him and gave him food and water. Deep in his heart he knew that Sniffles was his best friend. But one morning, when Dirk opened the back door, Sniffles didn't come running to say good morning as usual. No, Sniffles kept lying in his kennel and peered at Derek with tired little eyes. Derek's father took him to school and told him not to worry, he himself would take Sniffles to the vet immediately. Dirk was very worried and spent the day thinking about his best friend. When Derek's father came to fetch him, he gave Derek the sad news that Sniffles had died of tick fever. Derek's heart was broken and he often cried about his dog. It seems as if no-one could understand how he felt.

But the wonderful news is: God is with us in our sad times and He understands how we feel. In

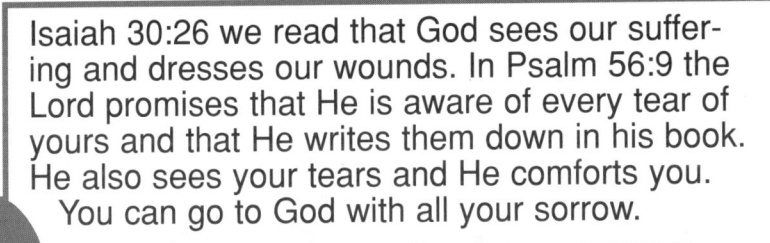

Isaiah 30:26 we read that God sees our suffering and dresses our wounds. In Psalm 56:9 the Lord promises that He is aware of every tear of yours and that He writes them down in his book. He also sees your tears and He comforts you.

You can go to God with all your sorrow.

> Lord, thank You for understanding my sorrow and for comforting me. Thank You that I may share all my troubles with You.

God is with you when you are sad and it is He who comforts you.

READ

Psalm 147:3 – He heals the brokenhearted and binds up their wounds.

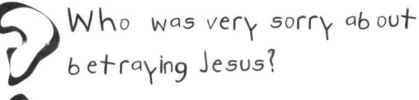

? Who was very sorry about betraying Jesus?

(Hint: Matthew 26:75)

ANSWER: Peter.

A promise that God will never leave you

Henry was a lively boy who could run very fast. He was happiest when he could play and run. His father always teased him and said that Henry ran before he could walk. When Henry went to school, he did well in athletics. He competed in almost all the meetings.

When Henry was only eight years old, he received provincial colours in athletics. He had to go on a tour to compete in the South African championships. Unfortunately his parents had already made other plans and couldn't accompany him on this tour. Henry was scared to travel without his parents. His father assured him that the Lord promises something wonderful in the Bible.

Psalm 16:8 promises you that the Lord is always with you to protect you. Never feel alone, because there always is Someone with you – God. Henry was holding onto this promise. And of course he had the most wonderful time of his life.

Even when you are alone or amongst strangers, you can have a wonderful time, because you know God is always with you.

> Lord, thank You that You are always with me. Thank You that I need never feel afraid.

The Lord is always with you. That is why you must not feel alone.

READ

Psalm 27:10 – Though my father and mother forsake me, the Lord will receive me.

? The Lord uses two things in nature to explain to you that He is always with you and will never leave you. What are these?

(Hint: Isaiah 43:2)

ANSWER: Rivers and fire